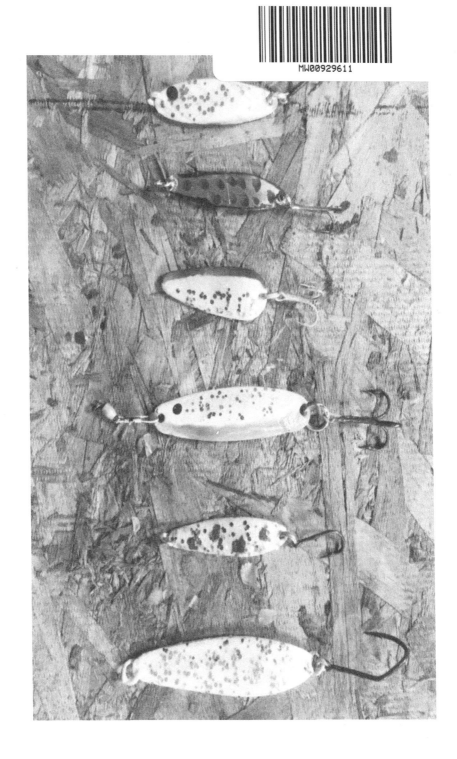

Life Rolls On

Moving on After Losing a Child to Addiction

Angie Gillette

In Loving Memory of Cody Gillette

<u>My Dearest Son</u>

You are my greatest wish come true,

Oh, how I love you!

With your eyes so blue,

And your smile so true.

I wish you peace in heaven from here on through.

Love Always ~ AG

This book is written to honor the memory of my dear son Cody

for being one of my life's greatest gifts and giving me strength.

For Duane and Kaylee for always being by my side.

To all of my family and friends for their kindness and support.

To the countless number of people who have suffered the pain

from losing a child, and those who have known or lost a loved

one struggling from addiction, depression and any form of

mental illness.

Foreword

Why Me God?

Why me God? That's the question I had asked myself over and over so many times. Why do I have to deal with so much? I try to live my life every day being kind and helping as many people as I can by doing good deeds, being a good listener, and never judging others. Just helping others and always being honest are my character traits that I live by. I believe wholeheartedly in the Golden Rule and try to lead by example wherever I go. Yet, I lived in a secret life of hell. That's my payback? Why? As an educator, I am blessed to be able to help so many children, but I couldn't save my own son. Why? How do I live with that?

Well, I now know. Though my faith may have wavered over the past ten years, I haven't lost it. I'm not sure that I agree with God's why, but I am driven for some reason to share my story. There are a lot of questions that I know will forever remain unanswered. A lot of guilt and what-ifs to ponder, but this I do know, some things were God's plan all along and we may never know the answers, nor the why for reasons that only He knows. Therefore, any time spent thinking about what could have been different and on blame is time wasted. It is best to try to accept God's will and move on the best that you can.

I have been given a purpose and even though I was only able to share a short time with my son (twenty-six years, two months, and two days) to be exact, I hope that I can bring others peace

and maybe save some from the crisis that many of us are dealing with – addiction. I am not embarrassed to write about it, nor am I ashamed of my son. I am proud of him for the courage and strength he had to share his battle with me and try as hard as he could to overcome it. Even though he lost the battle, I hope you read on to find out just how and why I have the strength – his strength to tell our story.

Contents

Chapter 1

Our Greatest Gift

" The most precious jewels you'll ever have around your neck

are the arms of your children." ~Anonymous

Our most precious gift in life is our children! I love children! I have always wanted to be around children. They make me happy. Ever since I can remember, I wanted to be a teacher and a mother. I couldn't wait to have children of my own.

Duane and I met through friends of ours. It was an instant attraction. We met in February around Valentine's Day at a party. After our first date, we were inseparable. We spent every day together and after a few months, he proposed in April. My mother was convinced that it was an April Fool's Day joke and was very concerned that I wouldn't finish college. However, I did complete my bachelor's degree in elementary education to become a teacher and went on to get a master's degree later when my kids were in high school to become a principal. Having a strong work ethic, strong commitment, and reaching goals are some of the few things that Duane and I have in common. Even though I married my total opposite, as I am writing this book, we have been married for 30 years. In fact, sometimes I wonder if we would have dated longer (like through hunting and fishing season), would I have still said yes? Would we have still gotten married? Now, I know that it happened that way because that was just another thing that was meant to be, because it was the destiny that created our amazing son.

We were married for about two years before I finally became pregnant with Cody. I used to cry and cry wanting a baby so bad. Like so many young couples, it was after I had given up and stopped thinking about getting pregnant when it finally happened. It wasn't the best timing actually, I was doing my student teaching and almost ready to graduate, plus working at the same time. The stress of wanting a baby so much had put a strain on our marriage, but then of course, it happened. It brought us close again.

It was a pretty easy pregnancy. I wasn't sick at all so, I gained sixty pounds craving and eating hostess cupcakes, which Cody also liked later on. I remember when I was getting close to my due date and Duane took me for a ride out west on some bumpy roads hoping to put me into labor (we read something about it – I think I drank castor oil too) to scout for something or other; I don't recall what, but it didn't put me into labor. The funny thing is that as Cody grew older, he would travel those same bumpy roads quite frequently hunting coyotes.

Well, on the night of December 6, 1991, a storm rolled in and my water broke at 1:30 AM. Off we rushed into Salt Lake City, nervous and excited at the same time. I had decided to go through natural childbirth. Why? I have no idea? It was cheaper on our insurance? So, no pain medication or epidural and twelve hours later at 3:41 PM in the afternoon I gave birth to one of my life's greatest gifts, Cody Richard Gillette.

I remember at first, he wasn't crying, and they took him aside really fast to clean out his lungs. He has a really raspy sound coming from him and he was trying his hardest to breathe and cry. Then the raspy sound turned into a regular cry and they brought him to me. From that moment on I have felt the greatest love of all, and my heart was full of warmth every time I heard any sound from him. Little did I know how precious the sound of a child's voice is even their cry. Now, I long to hear his voice again. Think whatever you want, but every morning since he passed away, as I drink my coffee during my few minutes of alone time, I play an album of photos and videos that I have created on my phone just to see his smile and hear his voice.

Having a child is truly a miracle. They are our greatest gift. Please take the time to really treasure every moment that you have with your children. Slow down and cherish them. Live in the moment. Take it all in. Give them your full attention, listen, observe, and enjoy! Build memories. Focus on the details. Smile and laugh. Most of all LOVE!

December 6, 1991, was one of the happiest days of my life and that feeling can never be taken away.

Chapter 2

Eyes So Blue

" There's a boy who stole my heart, he calls me mom"

~Anonymous

Cody was a very good baby. He wasn't fussy at all. He almost slept through the night from the very beginning. In fact, maybe I spoiled him right from the start, never wanting to put him down. I would go in to check on him at night to make sure that he was alright and just stare at him, tickle his face, or even pick him up and rock him even when he was asleep. I was so happy to have my precious gift.

I don't recall where Duane was one night a few months after

Cody was born, I think delivering water in St. George, but I remember sitting in the rocking chair with him staring down into his beautiful blue eyes and he was looking up at me staring back.

My heart was over pouring with love for this wonderful child that I was holding in my arms. I'm not much of a singer at all, but it was just the two of us so, as I sat there thinking about all of the hopes that I had for his future, I started to sing...

I love my Cody

Yes, I do!

I love my Cody

With his eyes so blue.

I love my Cody

Yes, I do!

I love my Cody

With his cute smile too.

I love my Cody

Yes, I do!

I love my Cody

I will always be here for you!

I love my Cody

Yes, I do!

I would tickle his cheeks and forehead while he looked up at me smiling. I continued to look down into those blue eyes that reminded me of the color of the clear blue ocean in Mexico, and I was so thankful to be blessed with the most beautiful baby ever. My mind continued to race with the dreams that I had for my son like I'm sure every mother does. I wanted him first and foremost to be happy. I wanted him to be an honest and kind person. I wanted him to be well liked and to be respectful. I wanted him to be a hard worker like his father and me. I wanted him to be helpful, loving, and caring. I wanted him to be smart and good at sports. Wow, that's a lot of wants. When it came right down to the last few years before he passed away, ALL I REALLY WANTED WAS FOR HIM TO BE HAPPY! I longed for times to see him smile. He did smile those last six months before he died as he did so often throughout his childhood.

Cody tried to be all of these things that I had wished for him and he was in many ways! Some of them I didn't find out about until recently that I will share with you later. Well, those are a lot of expectations and we didn't expect Cody to be perfect and we certainly aren't perfect parents. We tried our best. In fact, we are probably guilty of enabling him, giving him too many things and doing too much for him. We tried to teach him the right values and to work hard. Anyone that knows us, knows that we both have a strong work ethic and integrity. We do not have a perfect marriage, but we have a good one and set a good example for him.

However, that beautiful blue-eyed child that was so full of life and excitement being raised in a home full of love, happiness, praise, and patience (again not always perfect, but normal whatever that is) for some reason; would later lose his self-esteem and confidence therefore, turning to drugs and turning everyone's life upside-down. Changing everyone's hopes, dreams, and happiness. Then for a time, I became a mother looking into those same blue eyes with my heart still overflowing with love, but at the same time great sorrow, guilt, fear, regret, and uncertainty. The eyes that used to be as clear as the most beautiful sea filled with comfort and joy looking back at mine became cloudy and dazed filled full of lies, pain, fear, guilt, and regret.

For a little while, the hopes and dreams came back and so did my son. In the last six months of his life, I was able to look into his eyes and see some flickers of happiness. The clouds had disappeared. Truth. Goals. We spent more time together as a family again. Cody and I spent time together talking and watching movies. We were Netflix buddies. I got to see him smile more often and he was happy. We went to Disneyland as a family in early June of 2017. We had gone when the kids were younger around seven and eight, but they claim that they didn't remember it. So, off we went again. Plus, Duane, Kaylee, and I are Yankees fans and Cody is an Angels fan and the Yankees happened to be playing the Angels in Anaheim. We decided to drive and stop in Vegas for one night.

We also went fishing at Flaming Gorge twice that summer.

Duane, Cody, and I went to Vegas again in November for a concert. Duane and I had been going out to dinner every Friday night and Cody started to go with us. It was great having him do things with all of us again instead of not being home or not coming out of his bedroom.

Those times reminded me of when he was younger and even brought me back to that night while rocking and singing to him, we formed a deep bond that could never be broken. We had a strong connection and I always had a sense of when he needed me, or something was going to happen. And the worst thing ever happened the night of March 1, 2018, but for some strange, unknown reason that only God knows, I wasn't there for him. I broke my promise from the song that I sang to him all those years ago when he was young.

However, you will find out later our bond has never been broken.

I love my Cody

Yes, I do!

I love my Cody

With his eyes so blue.

I love my Cody

Yes, I do!

I love my Cody

With his cute smile too.

I love my Cody

Yes, I do!

I love my Cody

I will always be here for you!

I love my Cody

Yes, I do!

Chapter 3

The Best Brother

"Those we love don't go away; they walk beside us every day."

~ Unknown

Cody and Kaylee were about eighteen months apart. However, because of the way that their birthdays fell, his in December and hers in July, in school they were only a year apart. From the moment we told Cody that he was going to have a little sister, he was so excited and that never changed! He loved her so very much before he even met her. He would kiss my pregnant belly, lay his head on it, and talk to it. I bought him is own doll to take care of so that we could practice taking care of his baby "sissy."

I will never forget the day that we brought her home and let him hold her for the first time. The look on his face is imprinted in my mind forever. He was so happy! He would hold her, feed her, make sure that she had toys to play with. There was a time when I wasn't sure if Kaylee would ever walk or talk because Cody would do everything for her. They had their sibling moments like all children do such as poking at each other and not wanting to do the same thing or share. Cody always wanted to be near her and hugging on her or touching her and Kaylee is not a touchy person. She needs her space so, at times she would scratch his face in frustration. He even continued this up until his final days by walking by her and giving her a little poke or hug. He loved her so much.

It's interesting to me how parents can raise children in the same household with the same (I think they try anyway) parenting skills and the children are very different. I always wonder about this and I agree that we are all somewhat "products" of our environment and that certain factors can change us, but I really believe more so that it has to do with genetics and God has a plan for us before we are even born. That's why we need to love and accept our children and people for who they are. Sometimes those factors either environmental or genetic do not come into play until later in life. My children were totally opposite. I love them both very much for who they are. Cody was a very social child when he was younger and made friends so easily. He was outgoing, a leader, funny, a risk-taker, innovative, thoughtful, confident, and had very positive self-esteem. When he was around thirteen things changed and he became less social, not very confident, and had very low self-esteem. Kaylee was a very shy child. When she was younger, she would hide by me and cling to my leg when people came around. She would suck on her bottom lip always being afraid. She later became very social and confident. She was and still is resilient and has positive self-esteem. She has very strong will power for example, she can say she will give up cookies for a year and stick to it even when nobody is around. Cody did not have that resiliency, maybe that is something knowing what I know now about growth mindset, that I could have done a better job trying to teach him. Kaylee was also very independent and still is. She has always been very content at entertaining herself and not letting things bother her. She is her own person and does things at her own pace. At home

Cody was always by my side, he always wanted to be around me or know where I was. Kaylee would play in her room for a long time by herself just fine. However, neither of them would ever leave my side in public places.

At first, Cody loved school. Kaylee did not want to go to preschool, but Cody let his sissy know that it would be okay because he would be there to hold her hand. He made sure to teach his sister everything like fishing, hunting, and how to play night games like kick-the-can. They would sing karaoke and dance to 'NSYNC and The Backstreet Boys. They had a lot of the same neighborhood friends and school friends. Later on, secondary school became a battle for Cody and Kaylee went on to graduate from college. He was very proud of his smart and beautiful sister. In the later years, the dark times, I know that he wanted to remain close, but it was more than Kaylee could handle. He would ask me sometimes, "Why does my sister hate me?" She tried to help him, I know, as there were many times that she stayed up talking with him trying to help him, but it became too much, and everyone deals with addiction differently. She was in the basement in the bedroom right next door to him so, I'm sure that she saw and heard more than we did, and she didn't share it with us until later after Cody died, we all sat down and had a talk that helped us understand each other and relieve our guilt. Kaylee always thought that I favored Cody and that he was my "favorite" child. They were both somewhat jealous of the other. I always told her that a mother does not have a favorite child, she loves all of her children equally and with her whole heart! It was during this talk that I think she was able to finally understand that this was true. I told her there were times that Cody needed me more and in different ways, but that didn't mean I loved her less and she said that she knows that now. What a hard role we play as parents! I know there were times that Cody felt like a failure and that we loved Kaylee more because she had a job and he didn't even though I reassured him of the same things that I had told her. I was proud of them both and I wanted them both to be happy. We were willing to help both of them with what they needed to succeed in life. He said and did some awful things that he doesn't even know that he did, but they are not easily forgotten when someone is hurt. Her way of dealing with it was to ignore him, be angry, not include him, shut him out, or not help him with rides. We all understand that this was heartbreaking for Kaylee to lose her only sibling, a brother that had always taken care of her and supported her. She now knows and can live with the comfort that he is in peace. Cody had wanted to be that big brother, who took care of her just like he did so well when they were younger. He tried really hard, but he failed and for that I know deep in my heart he is very sorry. He loved her more than anything and will always be with her smiling down on her with love and pride. It is a bond that will also never be broken.

This was Kaylee's speech at Cody's funeral…

I just wanted to say a couple of things about my brother. In my opinion, I would say that God's greatest gift is his having a brother. Cody has been by my side since before I was born. He helped me in so many ways. Some of you knew me when I was little so, you can verify that I barely said 3 words. Cody helped me come out of my shell. Cody and I are 18 months apart in age. When we went to preschool I wouldn't go unless Cody was there with me, so he ended up staying with me another year. I wish my mom would have let him stay another year cause then when my grandma forgot me, I wouldn't have been so terrified because I would've had my big bro by my side.

My dad's love of the outdoors passed on to Cody and they both tried to pass it on to me. It worked for a couple of years but then I decided to be more of a girl. I remember the first time they took me rabbit hunting and I "shot" my first rabbit, but I can guarantee it was really Cody because he was more excited than I was he was screaming, yelling, and jumping on me. However, I think it was really Cody who shot it unless my rapid-fire style paid off.

I remember sitting in a backyard duck blind and yelling "Take em!" Then London and I on all fours pretending to be deer, and Cody shooting us with a fake bow and arrow. Then with the peeing in my waders and my love of animals hunting was just too much for me!

Growing up in the horseshoe we had the best times playing backyard baseball with Gage and Karlee and my mom taught us how to play kick the can with all the neighbors. Another fond memory was being added to the workforce before I even knew what that meant. Cody would send me and London up to the golf course with some golf balls and told us to sell as many as we could and he would be right back leaving us with the hard work while he went home to eat a pizza with mom.

The older I got, the more protective he got of me, being upset when I got my first boyfriend just making sure this kid was okay for his little sis. He continued to analyze any guy I talked to. His first question was always "does he hunt?" Little do both Cody and my dad know, I actually look for a guy that doesn't hunt.

One thing about myself is that I think I am pretty good at keeping secrets, but Cody never kept secrets from me. He could never go without telling me something, like when our dog would poop in the house, he made sure to tell me before my mom with that one. This past Christmas, my mom was surprising me with Yankee vs Houston tickets and Cody couldn't keep that secret he told me that morning we woke up. Cody, mom is making me go to the game this summer and just know I'll wear your ugly Angels shirt under my Yankees jersey and play your recording that you made saying, "Let's go Yankees," just for me. Don't get mad at me for playing this video of you cheering for my team.

Cody,
Thank you for being you! Thank you for making me laugh! Thank you for protecting me! Thank you for being my brother! I love you!

Chapter 4

Full of Life

" Blessed are the curious, for they shall have adventures"

~Lovelle Drachman

As I said before, Cody was a very happy and content baby! He didn't cry or fuss. He was what I call a blue personality with some yellow especially later in life and with the influence of alcohol or drugs. Those of you familiar with the color code of personality traits may know what I am talking about for those of you that don't here is a short explanation... he was blue in that he was always sensitive to the needs of others, motivated by intimacy and relationships, compassionate, but worried a lot. Yellow in that he was sociable, charismatic, also, later on with ADHD and anxiety he was impulsive, disorganized, unfocused, and spontaneous.

He always wanted to be by my side. We were literally attached at the hip. I would cook and clean carrying him. As I said, he was content and happy, but wanted my attention. He had his pacifier and bottles until he was almost two until we told him that the birds swooped down and took them. We had to drive around and look for about a week after. We tried to make sure to give him all of the experiences in life that we could; the zoo, reading to him, swimming lessons, preschool, Sunday school, hunting, fishing, and teaching him everything that we could.

He was a smart baby. He walked before he was a year old and talked early. One of his first words besides mama and dada was duck. Sure, he was spoiled. He was my parents' first grandchild and Duane's parents' other grandchildren lived in Arizona so, he was the one that lived close by. They all were more than willing to babysit whenever we needed them. Duane's mom eventually ended up babysitting both Cody and Kaylee six months after I went back to work, and my sitter quit. He had an amazing bond with all of his grandparents.

I remember the first time my dad saw Cody when he was born, and he came to the hospital. He was so happy that he cried. My dad taught him to golf when he could first walk with little plastic clubs and loved to talk about baseball with him. Cody, in my opinion, looked like my dad as he got older and they had very similar behaviors. My dad is a very kind, compassionate, and caring man. He does have some insecurities about his self-esteem just like Cody did. My dad is an alcoholic and Cody really struggled with this. He totally disapproved of his behavior and didn't want much to do with him as he grew older. I think deep down he knew that he suffered from an addiction the same way and it was too hard to watch another person that you love struggle and do that to them self, knowing that you were doing the same thing. I often felt like I was seeing the same person in fact, I watched my younger brother, struggle with addiction as well. He lived most of his adult life away from Utah so, Cody did not know him, but their behaviors were so very similar. This all goes back to my thoughts on addiction being a hereditary disease.

Later on, a month before Cody died, I had been staying up late with him watching movies, talking, and just being there for him and one Sunday he returned the favor and was there for me at a time when no one else was. I had just come from cleaning my dad's house and taking him some food and I went straight past Cody, who was in the family room watching TV, to my bedroom and broke down crying. My dad had started to lose his memory and wasn't doing very well. Cody came in and talked me through it and was so supportive and caring. It was like he was the only one who understood what I was going through and how to comfort me. This was something that I could never talk to Duane and Kaylee about. I will always be thankful that he was there for me that day. It was like I had the old kind and compassionate Cody back right by my side. We were so close those last few months. I will treasure every memory of every moment we had. There is a saying on Facebook that I've seen about teaching your kids to talk to you honestly when they are young so that they will continue to do it when they are older. Well, I always told my children to do that and oh boy, have I been told many things that a parent does not want to hear, but I did not judge nor, did it make me love them less. I tried my best to not show my hurt, but only to listen and help. I just wish some things that Cody told me had been said sooner so, I could have helped sooner. Perhaps, maybe some of the times in his earlier teenage years I could have really listened better rather than lectured and preached?

Grandma Janice...oh how she loved Cody! She was always so concerned about her Codeman! They also had a special bond. She was right there from the moment he was born. In fact, since I'm pretty much telling all in this book, why not add a little humor/embarrassment, she was literally right there waiting for Cody to be born. I was in my hospital bed and the doctor was doing a check to see how far I was dilated then mentioned that she could see Cody's head so, my mom pushed her way in an sat beside the doctor with her McDonald's cheeseburger like Johnny Bench waiting for the play at home plate.

Some of Cody's favorite times when he was younger were going back to South Dakota to visit my parents' relatives. We would often stay at my maternal grandparent's house on Lake Madison. Talk about being full of life...that was Cody. He was the oldest of the great-grandchildren. He would fish all day and night. He was in all of his glory. One time he caught the biggest carp that I have ever seen in my life! He carried it up from the lake like a baby and everyone cheered. He would take them all on little treasure hunts through the trees and cornfields. All of the second cousins would follow Cody chanting, "We're going on a treasure hunt, we're going on a treasure hunt."

Cody had many adventures with Duane's mom and dad when he was young as well when he got older. His grandpa would often take him fishing to Flaming Gorge. He would go camping and to Yellowstone with them and grandpa would tell him and Kaylee bigfoot and werewolf stories. When they were at home in Utah, they would build fires in the fireplace and eat popcorn. They supported him in all of his sports and everything that he did. Sherron would call him every day when he was older to say "Hi" and check on him.

Cody loved other children and he played well with them. He would organize games and events in the neighborhood. The kids would play baseball in the front yard. He loved Barney! I took him to the grocery store once when they had Barney there. I wasn't sure if he would sit in the chair by Barney because he might be too scared, but when he saw Barney, he ran up to him and kissed him. hugged him and wouldn't let go. I had to pull him away crying. He would dance and sing to Barney all of the time.

Cody was very hands-on and busy all of the time. He would mow the lawn with his dad and grandpas. He would drive his Bigfoot truck, the boat, and anything his dad would let him. I loved it when we went camping and he would go off on his four-wheeler only to come back in just a few minutes to bring me flowers. He was always bringing me flowers. He would hook up his bike to his wagon with a ton of rope and drive it around the block to look for treasures (mostly scraps of wood to build his treehouse with), or to go fishing with.

The treehouse...oh my, what a creation that was! It had wood, carpet, and a ton of nails. I remember when he was finished and asked me to come sit in it, nails were going every which way, but of course we were both proud.

He always wanted a fishing pond in the backyard. Every spring he would build one. He loved to sing and had a very beautiful voice. One of our favorite memories is when he was about four years old and Santa brought him a play electric guitar for Christmas. He was so excited saying, "Look daddy, a guitar, a guitar!" Also, when he was older and we got the karaoke machine and guitar hero he would sing like he was Kid Rock, Tim McGraw, Eminem, Tom Petty, or The Backstreet Boys. He could play the guitar like Eddie Van Halen for sure! He also loved to rollerblade and skateboard and became really good at that. Of course, with that came a new building project of building ramps and half-pipes that covered the street for the neighborhood kids to use. He did bike tricks on the same ramps as well. Oh and I cannot forget the Kawasaki 80 dirt bike. When he first got it, it was so cute! He would ride it in circles around the globe willow tree in the front yard for hours. I recently found out that one day after school he tried to teach Kaylee to ride it and she ran into the house and the fence. I am the only one that did not know about this event. Everyone kept it a secret. He always made sure that his little sissy knew how to do everything and was always there to teach her and support her.

Chapter 5

Special Times

"When someone you love becomes a memory, that memory becomes a treasure."

~Unknown

Like many mothers, I remember that first moment when I looked down at my newborn child for the first time and instantly formed a bond that is was so special it's hard to find the right words to express the feeling of complete exuberance and deep, unconditional love, for this sweet little bundle of joy that I am finally getting to meet. Of course, I thought he was the most beautiful baby ever, just as I did his sister when she was born.

In fact, with those blue eyes and darling face, I just had to put him in the local beauty pageants. I made sure that I dressed him cute, I am a shopper after all and they do have cute stuff for boys, too. With his fun, outgoing personality, he did well. There was one pageant that he won Mr. Photogenic and another where he won King.

When Cody was in his early elementary school years, he went to the same school that I taught at. It was great to have both of my kids at school with me. It was interesting, in kindergarten, he would change hands from left to right as to which one he wanted to write with. I thought for a while that he may end up being left-handed like his dad, but he decided on being right-handed. Also, he attended kindergarten when they were at the time of doing more of a whole language approach rather than phonics so, he would bring flashcards home to memorize words and if he passed the words off, he would get a book to read. This was a challenge. We would work on the words, get the book, but then he would forget the words. I am bringing all of this up because these are pieces of a puzzle that I should have put together much sooner than I did especially being an educator myself. There are many things that I have learned about reading recently that I wish I had known then. I may have been better able to help Cody. As I look back on many of the pieces of his academic puzzle, many things could have been done differently to possibly have helped him. Would it have made all of the difference? We won't know. I do know this; however mother's know. They have the intuition and specific knowledge of each of their children as to what is right and wrong. Just as when he was young and I took him to the doctor when I was sure that something was wrong and they sent me home saying it was "just a virus" only to go back a few days later with him having pneumonia. I knew. Always trust your motherly instinct! Always. You know. I should have trusted it more in academics and been more of an advocate for my son. Even if you don't know, keep observing and questioning. Cody struggled in reading and spelling.

In first grade at West Elementary, Cody won an award for the best book at Artists' and Authors' Night. It was about his hamster, Max. He continued on in school doing okay. He struggled with spelling and reading but was right on the edge of being on grade level/below grade level. He was a "bubble kid." Homework was a battle though. In third grade, we changed schools to Stansbury Park Elementary and for the next couple of years things continued the same. He had good teachers so, he was able to make it. He was full of energy. In fifth grade, he was chosen as Student of the Month.

It was my pleasure to be his teacher in the sixth grade. It was great. I was able to help him and to see his needs. I was a coach of a gifted program called Destination Imagination and he was on one of the teams. I consider this the 90's version of STEM education. This was right up his alley. It was hands-on learning, building and performing. Their challenge was to write a skit, build everything, set up in a certain amount of time and have a technical element in it. His team made a big screen TV and I remember when they performed, he had the crowd rolling with laughter. He was a leader in the classroom and had many great qualities as a student. However, I was still concerned about his spelling and reading. I asked about having him tested for SPED (special education). I was told he wouldn't qualify. Also, that year by having him in my class, it was very clear that he had ADHD (or so I thought then and I still do but knowing more of what I know now maybe more of it was anxiety). So, in talking with him and Duane, we took him to the doctor, did all of the tests and tried medication. It was amazing the focus that he had in school and how he was able to sit still, stay organized, not yell out, and overall perform better. He even noticed a difference himself and liked it. However, there were side effects...terrible stomachaches, he became aggressive in a mean way wanting to fight, which he had never done before, and my mother thought he wasn't the fun Cody anymore. It affected his appetite and he was already really skinny and one of the shortest kids in the class. We debated and weighed heavily on what to do. We decided to stop the medication and he didn't stay on the medication very long.

We maybe should have tried something else, or given it more time, who knows what was right, maybe we made a mistake. I have seen medications work with children and I have seen them fail. I do not give advice, nor do I judge because four years later we tried something else that may have been the decision that lead to his death? I will discuss this later.

We are a family that loves sports. At an early age Cody was golfing. My side of the family is all golfers as well as his dad. Duane played high school golf and so did my brother, my mom and dad worked at the golf course and we lived on the golf course so, it was only natural that he learn to play golf. Duane spent a lot of time with him teaching him to golf. When he was in eighth grade, Duane entered him in Drive, Chip, and Putt contests and he won the chipping contest. When he was a freshman and sophomore, he played for Grantsville High School's golf team. He was a good golfer. He struggled a bit with the anxiety and stress that the competition of the game can bring and then other things in his life took him down. He eventually quit the team.

We didn't have soccer when we were young, but our kids grew up in the soccer era. Soccer was the first sport that they could play on a team and at the youngest age (you can be four). So, wanting to give my son every opportunity, I signed him up for soccer and I was the coach for the first couple of years. It was fun. He liked soccer and he was a fast runner. I used to tease him sometimes saying that he was like Forrest Gump when we were sitting out in the front yard and he was running down the street. He kept playing soccer and ended up with an absolutely amazing soccer coach named Eddie Clements. Coaches are like teachers, when you get the good ones, who are truly inspirational, can see the talent in every kid, and know how to bring it out in them, it can be life-changing. They know how to build a relationship of mutual respect. Wow! Cody could play soccer. It wasn't a sport that we grew up with so, it took a while to understand and it can be boring and frustrating when there aren't many goals scored. However, it takes an awesome athlete to play soccer! You need to be extremely fit to run up and down that field. Cody was awesome. He would play the whole game. Eddie would yell out, "Gillette...Gillette..." for Cody to go get the ball from one end of the field to the other. He was able to play both defense and offense. As they grew older, with his running talent he played offense to score goals. I can still hear Coach Clements calling his name. Those were special times!

Then there's baseball, our favorite. It all started with tee ball. Duane was the coach. Fun times! That is some true entertainment. The next couple of years were busy for Duane at work so, he was able to be an assistant coach on a couple of the teams all the while working with Cody whenever they could. They had some great years with Duane coaching and assistant coaching. Cody played catcher, pitcher, first base, third base, shortstop and outfield. He had some good coaches and a couple where I had to drag him to practice and tell him that he couldn't be a quitter. I reminded him that he signed up and made a commitment so, he needed to stick with it for his team. We were new to the baseball scene as far as the regular league vs. the super league and I wish that we would have known more like we did when Kaylee played softball, perhaps that may have kept Cody playing longer.

Before he quit playing baseball however, he had the best years ever, when he was in sixth grade along came another one of those coaches that not only develop and foster talent, but help create true athletes and sportsman by teaching them the skills and characteristics that they need for life. This man was Steve Branch. Duane was an assistant coach that year and the Mariners were a fine example of a team. In fact, this was also the year that I was Cody's teacher. One of the assignments that I give is to write an autobiography. Kaylee and I recently came across Cody's in the closet and as we were reading it, for his future years he wrote about being a professional baseball player.

Cody was a pitcher that year. I loved to watch him pitch! It is a very nerve-wracking time, however when your child is the pitcher. Cody would walk the bases loaded a lot and then strike out the next three batters. One of the most exciting moments of my life was watching him pitch a no-hitter. We were all so proud of him! I know that both Duane and I miss watching both Cody and Kaylee play sports.

The next year, he moved up to the thirteen and under league and it was more challenging. That along with one of his best friends moving away, and the Stansbury kids going to junior high in Grantsville where there was a totally different culture even though they only lived ten miles away, ended Cody's baseball career. While Kaylee was able to find friends in Grantsville (she still has them today) and fit-in well, Cody didn't quite find his niche there. He didn't have the confidence in himself to continue to play baseball. At that time there wasn't a Stansbury team so, it was either play on a Tooele or Grantsville team. The teams in Grantsville were very close-knit with kids from Grantsville. He just didn't have high self-esteem to fit in. There was one of the main players on the team that he clashed with. So, he made friends that were not good influences on him. We should have invited them to our house more. We were used to having his friends over, knowing their parents, and knowing the kids well. Then it changed to him asking to stay after school in Grantsville and we trusted him, but we did not check up on the friends as we should have. In fact, he would tell me things and I was under the impression that they were really good friends, but one of them was into drugs.

Eddie Clements and Steve Branch attended Cody's funeral. I'm sure that meant a lot to him just as it did to me. Thank goodness the world has good people in it that can see the potential in everyone.

Chapter 6

The Legend

"Heroes get remembered, but legends never die"

~Max Holloway

From the moment Cody could walk and talk, he was hunting and fishing with his dad and grandpas. Some of his first words were duck and elk. He knew how to use a duck call and bugle for elk at an early age. I remember him winning a few contests. He would dress all up in whatever gear that he needed and load up his Bigfoot truck or wagon with hunting or fishing supplies.

I think his first hunting experience was probably pheasant hunting in Fillmore, Utah, being packed on his dad's back. Then deer hunting in the camper or scouting. I remember packing him on my hip when I shot my elk. There was a time when he must have only been let's say, younger than two and we were camping in the Uintah Mountains and I remember packing Cody on my hip again as we trekked through the mountains. Then he wanted to walk some on his own "like his dad" so, he and I were following Duane on the trails and Cody was having a blast. He was picking me flowers. He never took his eyes off of his dad and would copy whatever he did. He played in the dirt and looked for elk. Now, as for me, I wasn't having quite so much fun. That night the coyotes were howling, and I was scared to death (Cody wasn't) thinking what if something happened to Duane, I am out here with an almost two-year-old in the middle of nowhere and I do not know my way out, nor do I know how to drive a stick shift truck. Looking back now, and knowing what I know about Cody, he probably could have taken over as navigator even then. He was a natural. One of my favorite videos that I still play over and over just to hear his voice, is one that he has posted on his Utah Wild Boys Facebook page. He and one of his friends created the Facebook page as one of the steps toward becoming a fishing and hunting guide. He would post pictures on it every time he went fishing or hunting. He would encourage others to go on adventures and post as well. Duane and Kaylee have kept the page active after his passing. He is hiking in Wyoming and he gets to the top of a ridge and scans it for everyone to see and says, "That's God's country right there." He was known for his ability to hike anywhere at any time.

He loved to duck hunt and would make sure to instill that love in other youth. He would wait for the opening youth duck hunt and take other neighborhood kids on their first duck hunt teaching them how to hunt.

When he was in junior high, he wrote a letter for a contest to the Avery Pro Staff and won the contest to be on the Avery Youth Staff. It was very exciting. Duane and Cody went to Kansas on a "hunt of a lifetime" with Derek Rambo one of the Avery Youth Field Staff Managers, who was sponsoring the hunt for the purpose of listening to the fresh young minds that were the future of hunting. They had a blast.

Well, that's a little snippet of the hunting legend. There will be more to come in the best friend chapter with his dad. He knows more than me about the subject.

I want to share some fishing stories. My son was truly a remarkable fisherman! He was behind the wheel of the boat from a very young age sitting on daddy's or Grandpa Ron's lap. He would try to pull the boat with his Bigfoot truck. As I mentioned before, he would make a fishing pond in our back yard every spring. There are a few memories that stick out in my mind however that make me shake my head and smile. One is when he was four years old and I was getting him ready for swimming lessons, he didn't really want to go and his sister for sure did not want to go, she was extremely afraid of water, I bribed him yes, you read it right, I bribed him with fishing. I told him that if he got ready and got his stuff then after his lesson he could fish while Kaylee was having hers. We live in an area with a golf course, community pool, tennis courts, and a man-made lake. The pool was next to the lake. Well, that's all it took. He was ready. Well, I had started something because another time after lessons he wanted to fish, but we hadn't brought anything to fish with.

I should back-up a little and tell you about my own experience with fishing. I was not a fan. Both of my parents love to fish. My mom grew up on Lake Madison in South Dakota. They used to take my brothers and me fishing all of the time. It was always a miserable experience for me. We didn't have our own boat so, when we weren't using one of either of my grandpa's boats or fishing from shore, they would rent a canoe. Yes, I said a canoe. All five of us would go out in a canoe all day long to fish. My younger brother couldn't sit still to save his life. I was scared we would tip over. Who wants to touch a worm or a minnow to bait your line? Not me. It wasn't until later when I got to watch my son the expert fisherman, that I became a fan of fishing.

So, back to that day after lessons when we hadn't brought any gear to fish with. He wanted to just go by the lake and look for fish so, I let him. I could sit on the bench between the pool and the lake and watch both Kaylee and him. The next thing I know, he came back with a stick and some tangled up line with a hook on it. He rigged it up as a pole. He told me he was going to fish with that. I said, "okay, but Cody, it's just a bare hook." A few minutes later, he comes running over with a fish that he caught on the bare hook, line and a stick combo as excited as could be. I will never forget that day and I will cherish that memory forever!

Another fun time fishing was when we went to Lake Powell and he taught me how to clean a fish. We have that on video. It's quite funny. As much as Cody loved to fish, he would willingly give up his pole to teach someone else or give them the opportunity to catch one.

Kaylee told me a story about when he taught her to fish on Stansbury Lake, they went down the bank and he helped her cast her pole out telling her to just stand there and reel it in slowly and he would be right back. He walks down the bank a little way. A few minutes later she was screaming his name because she had a fish on and was being pulled in the water. So, Cody came running down the hill yelling at her to not let go. He would always get so excited as she said more excited than her. That is how she caught her first bass, which was huge.

He would continue to fish around Stansbury and when he was around ten years old, he caught a crappie that was just shy of the state record. You've already heard about the giant carp that he caught in South Dakota. He loved to take other people fishing and help them catch "the big one." He loved to teach little kids to fish. He would get so excited, whoop and holler, and his hands would shake. Those hands. I loved those hands. Always dirty. Always cracked. True little boy and then man hands. They often smelled like fish. I can still picture his long slender fingers and one of the last things I did when I left his side the day in the mortuary when I had the chance to sit alone with his body as it returned from the medical examiner after it had been ripped away from me was to trace his fingers and hold his hands in mine.

I often joked with Cody saying that I should have named him Hunter and he always said no, that I should have named him Fisher. I agree that would have been a very cool and appropriate name for him. I asked him once what made him such a great fisherman and he said,

" Mom, you have to talk to them and before you release them you give them a little kiss." I started to pay more attention and sure enough, he did these things. In my talk at his funeral, I called it the "Cody Gillette Secret."

Cody always wanted to make a career out of being a hunting or fishing guide and we were trying to help him with that. He would have been awesome at it. It was his passion. Unfortunately, he was gone too soon before his dream could come true. However, his fishing and hunting skills were legendary and those that he taught will never forget their time spent with him and what they learned from him.

Cody Richard Gillette

December 6, 1991-March 1, 2018

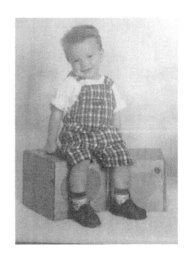

Chapter 7

Best Friends

"Death ends a life, not a relationship."

~ Mitch Alborn

It's easy for that bond between a mother and child to form while the baby is in the mother's womb, but it occurred for Duane and Cody even before Cody was born as well. I recall Duane with his hands upon my belly talking to Cody. Duane would read hunting books to Cody when he was just a few months old. He would watch fishing or hunting videos on television while holding Cody in his lap teaching him to "bugle like an elk" or 'make a call like a duck."

From the time Cody could walk, he was fishing and hunting with his dad. Duane took Cody pheasant hunting in Fillmore when he was around two years old carting him around in a backpack on his back. They had their "lucky spots" that they would always go for hunting every year. They would pack up and go to Fillmore or Richfield and carry on the tradition of the annual deer hunt.

In Cody's younger years, I would go along too. I wasn't about to let my young son go into the wilderness alone! Truth be told, one of my greatest fears is being lost in the wilderness. I would take city life with millions of people any day over the vast wilderness without anyone around. There was that one time that we went camping in the Uintah Mountains and several other deer hunts. However, as Cody got older, I stayed home and I'm sure that they had a lot more fun and their bond grew deeper. I knew Cody was in good hands with Duane because I would see the pictures like the one where he had Cody so bundled up that he looked like the Pillsbury Dough Boy so, I knew he would never be cold.

I used to really enjoy the times before a hunting or fishing trip while sitting around the family room listening to them make their big plans and look at maps together. Or when they would come back from one of their adventures, Cody would be so excited to tell about the fish that were caught or the animal that was bagged. I always secretly hoped that whatever trophy they brought home wasn't big enough to be mounted because then all I could think about was dollar signs and oh my, where are we going to hang that??

They had some unforgettable hunts like the one when Cody was on The Avery Youth Staff and they went to Kansas to goose hunt, or when they would go to Colorado to deer and elk hunt. They went to Wyoming deer hunting. They became dedicated hunters and were able to hunt archery, muzzleloader, and rifle seasons. Cody would practice bow hunting in the back yard (there are a few holes in my vinyl fence that made me upset, but now I look at them and smile). He has a 25 inch 4pt. deer still in velvet mounted that he was really excited about.

I remember when Cody wanted to start coyote hunting and Duane would help him research the best calls and equipment. Cody aka Davy Crockett with his coonskin hat later really got into coyote hunting and trapping. He was going to make me a coat one day. He would play that coyote call in the house and that is an awful sound! What a kid! We sure miss him!

Then there was turkey hunting. We went camping in our trailer one time up into the canyon with the Andersons our family friends so, they could all turkey hunt because that's where they had the tags and even as a teenager, Cody was full of fun and life. Dancing around camp like Steveo. He kept us all entertained that trip. Another little secret of mine is that I am scared of birds. Shortly after Cody passed away, his wonderful friend and taxidermist called to let us know that his turkey that he mounted was finished. So, Duane and I went in to pick it up and on the way home… turkey in the back seat, me in the front seat, Duane slams on the brakes and the turkey face/beak come flying forward right at me! I'm sure Cody was laughing at that one!

Duane and Cody had been to Colorado once. It was Cody's first big game hunt when he was twelve. Cody had the time of his life. They had been planning to go back before Cody died. This last fall, Duane went with Kevin and Kanyon Anderson. I know it was hard for Duane, but I know Cody was smiling down on them. Cody was very special to Kanyon and Kevin. Kevin is like a second dad to him. They love him very much. Duane had given Kevin a pair of Cody's hunting boots. They were elk hunting and on the opening day of the hunt about five minutes after daylight, Kevin shot a six by six elk. It was amazing.

Fishing. Fishing trips were perhaps Duane and Cody's best times. Fishing was Cody's

passion. I truly believe that some people are born with natural abilities and talents and that some people are meant to do certain things. Cody was meant to fish. I wish that he could have fulfilled his dream of being a fishing guide. When he was young, we used to call him Bill Dance and tell him he could have his own fishing television show one day. He would tie his Bigfoot truck up to Duane's boat and try to pull it and then when he was a little older, he would rig up his wagon to his bike with fishing poles and all of the gear he needed and go over to the lake in Stansbury to fish. He made friends with a lady that lived on the lake and fished from her dock. This became his "secret spot" and that's where he caught a huge crappie, just barely missing the state record at that I mentioned earlier.

Duane and Cody liked to fish at Strawberry Reservoir, Vernon, Pineview, and of course, Flaming Gorge. They made many trips fishing.

Cody would always out fish Duane. However, Duane mostly liked to fish for the big lake trout while Cody liked more of the fast action of the kokanee salmon and bass. Whatever they were fishing for didn't matter however, what mattered was that they were out on the water doing what they loved making memories with each other. Those were the times that Cody was happy. He would talk. He would smile. He could enjoy life. I remember Duane telling me that he loved his times fishing with Cody. He would tell me that he too, loved to see the smile on Cody's face and see him come to life when he was out on the water doing what he loved. There's something relaxing and calming about being out on the water. You are at peace. They had many great talks out on the water. I'm so glad. There's a peacefulness and serenity. I was worried that Duane would never want to take the boat out and fish again with Cody gone, but thankfully some of our friends have filled in and he is still fishing.

Cody also liked to go night fishing on the Jordan River for catfish. He also liked to fish all night at Grantsville Reservoir. He had a small boat with an electric motor that he would take out on Stansbury Lake. A couple more of my favorite videos to watch are ones of him fishing because they show his excitement. He says things like, "Yeah baby, that's a big one." and "Cha Ching." You can hear him laugh. I will always treasure those memories and I am so glad that we have him on video fishing.

Duane also taught Cody all about sports. He taught him to golf. He taught him all about baseball and how to be an amazing pitcher. I loved to watch Cody play and it was awesome to have Duane be a part of the time when he pitched the no-hitter as one of the coaches.

There were times during the "dark times" when Duane wasn't very understanding and Cody felt it. I think he felt disappointed in himself and lived with excruciating pain and guilt that he had let us down and disappointed us. There were times that he said to me, " My dad doesn't like me." Duane was like many millions of other people that are under the assumption or belief that addiction is a choice and not a disease. He would admit to me that he just didn't understand why Cody just didn't quit doing drugs. Cody knew this and would say that his dad just thought he was a drug addict, or take Duane's words and twist them. Duane no longer thinks the same way.

Cody pawned a lot of Duane's things. Sadly, he got blamed for pawning things that we later found. He also lost a lot of Duane's things.

Of course, this upset Duane, but Duane truly doesn't care about things.
He only cared about Cody. He would have done anything to help Cody
and to save Cody.

There was a time when Cody was on something, I'm not sure
what, but as I've researched and done my own investigating (too late) I
believe it to be a combination of things, including Xanax. I think that
when he would take Xanax, which is a benzodiazepine and I believe our
next major American epidemic, he would become agitated, full of rage,
hostile, have hallucinations/paranoia, not be able to sleep, then cry and
be suicidal. Then the next day he did not remember any of it. During
one of the incidents he wanted to kill Duane with a baseball bat.
However, most of the times his anger and agitation were directed
toward me; he would say awful things to me about what a terrible
mother I was, throw things at me, and tell me that he hated me, and
Duane was the one talking to him while he was sobbing. Duane was
always there for him. Actually, we all were at different times. In the late,
late nights and early mornings it was Kaylee, most of the other times
Duane, in the last year before he died it was me. None of us ever gave
up, we just made it through in our own ways. Even, through all of that
Duane was the one that was always willing to help no matter what. He

would say, "I'll sell everything that I own to get him help." He did not want to lose his son!

Through all of this, Cody would always say to me, "My dad is my best friend." He was very sincere when he would say it. I hope that Duane knows that! I'm sure that he does now. I know that he misses him, but I know that Cody is by his side.

Chapter 8

Dark Times

ADDICTION
is the easiest thing in the world
to have an opinion about,
But the hardest thing in the world
to go through.

"Grow through what you go through"

~Eric Butterworth

We went through some very hard times in our lives that I'm sure many people didn't even know about. We did the best that we could. Yes, we made many mistakes as I'm sure some of you reading will agree. As you read this chapter, please try not to judge, but hopefully understand a little bit. Maybe you will and maybe you won't, but I feel compelled to tell my story. There are so many things that could have and/or should have been done differently, but sadly we cannot go back in time. It has to be written because it is part of the story. I am putting our family's dark secrets out into the open for several reasons; maybe it will help other families that are struggling with some of the same things to get help, maybe others can learn and not make the same mistakes that we did, to educate people, for other parents/families that have gone through this to find comfort in the fact that they are not alone, for others to know that they aren't the only ones that tried that and failed, for people to know that they are not alone, and that there is always hope.

Thinking back, I'm not exactly sure when everything went downhill. Things start to change between teenagers and parents as teens pull away a bit and want to become more independent and private. That is natural. There were many events leading up to a time in Cody's life when I think things changed. We had always been a close family and encouraged our kids to do the right things. Because of our difference in religion, we didn't attend church as we should have. I tried, but it was hard to take two little children on my own. I should have done better, that is no excuse. It was also hard for my kids being Lutheran which was not the predominant religion in Utah. When you reach junior high all of those things come into play. We had instilled values into our children and encouraged them to be honest with us.

They knew that they could talk to us about anything, but I think there was still that, shall I say embarrassment or fear of disappointment in telling your parents everything. I don't remember talking to my parents and telling them everything when I was a teenager. I think that no matter how much you know that your parents love you unconditionally it's still kind of a rite of passage to make some wrong choices and do some stupid things as a teenager. It's almost like it's a fact of life. A necessity of growing up. It's part of the plan. Most all of us can think back on things that we said or did that make us wonder how we didn't get hurt or in trouble. Some of these things are regrets and some are learning experiences. I think that those of us parenting millennials have tried to have a much more open relationship with our children due to the society that we live in and the challenges that our children face at younger ages. The expectation is one of such that we have raised our children to feel more comfortable to come to us.

For Cody, there certainly weren't any major factors that some people in society think are the reasons teenagers turn to drugs like poverty, poor education, single parents, divorce, abuse, parents with addiction, or severe trauma. There were no ACEs-Adverse Childhood Experiences. As an educator, I have taken the quiz, studied child development and psychology. There was no abuse, no neglect, and no major household challenges. Sadly, Cody is not the only young man that I am seeing this happen to that didn't have any of these factors. It is happening more and more.

However, here are the many factors that I believe contributed to Cody's addiction: genetics, mental health issues like early adulthood depression, ADHD, a learning disability, our school system failed him, friends moving away, poor self-esteem, anxiety, enablement from parents, abandonment from friends, heartbreak from relationships, and it was just God's plan. I will now take the time to explain. I want to make it very clear before I proceed that I do not blame anyone for my son's circumstances or death and that nobody should blame themselves for anything. Cody would not want that.

That first summer after sixth grade, my grandma passed away. We planned to go back to South Dakota for the funeral. Cody did not want to go. That was a little different, but he was almost thirteen. It was a long drive, which we all dreaded since we always drove straight through. We weren't going for a vacation, but rather a funeral. He loved going to South Dakota, but I let him stay home with Duane. Then in the fall, he started junior high in Grantsville. Stansbury Park did not have a junior high so, our kids rode the bus to Grantsville. This was an interesting cultural mix. I love Grantsville. It is where I have spent much of my career. It is a small friendly town known for farming and has a cowboy-like feel. It is a very close- knit community, but growing and changing now. Stansbury Park was and still is known as a more affluent community and the kids were considered rich snobs. As I mentioned before, Kaylee made the transition easily and made a lot of friends that she still has today. Unfortunately, one of Cody's best friends moved that year to Salt Lake City and playing sports became a little harder to break into the "hometown boys" of Grantsville. Cody didn't have the confidence. I remember when I was that age, it was when I first moved to Utah so, I get it. I went through kind of the same thing. I went from having a close group of friends to not knowing anyone and I remember feeling shy and scared. I made friends in different groups. It's kind of sad that even today, we have our so-called groups or cliques in junior high and high school. Kids go from elementary school where they all play together, accept each other and help each other to junior high and high school where they are in almost separate societies with their own rules and norms. So, a kid who was well-liked by everyone in elementary can suddenly <u>not</u> fit in at all; and a kid that could do okay academically

getting by because the teachers are there to closely monitor him, can

suddenly become lost and doesn't know what to do for help.

Cody fell in with the wrong crowd. I realized this a few years too

late. He would tell me all about his friend and the things he would say

had me thinking what a nice kid he was, I should have been more

involved like I was with his other friends. This kid lived in Grantsville

though and he didn't invite him over. He just hung out with him at

school and activities. As I mentioned before, I trusted him. I had no

reason not to. School was a struggle, in junior high I was called once

because his shirt was not tucked in so, I told him to tuck his shirt in. It's

unfortunate that the focus was on shirts being tucked in and not on how

to help him academically. There was another time when he wasn't

allowed in class because he didn't have a pencil. Really? I remember

going to Parent/Teacher Conferences in eighth grade and we went into

his English teacher's class and the teacher was very positive, then we

turned the corner and the line was out the door and down the hall to go

into the next teacher's class. Cody refused to go in with me. When I

went in, I totally understood why, I introduced myself as Cody Gillette's

mom and was greeted with a smirk. I was taken aback. I sat down as the teacher did while she slapped three stacks of paper on the table and said, "Crap, Crap, and more Crap." I was in shock. No wonder Cody didn't want to come into the conference. I was appalled later by what he told me about the things she said and did to other students. Teachers like that have no business being in the profession. It saddens me that she taught in my district and taught my children. I did call the principal and let him know.

The next year in high school, I asked again for him to be tested for special education, but I was again told that he did not qualify. I am so stupid. I am so well educated on the special education process and laws now that I will never let this happen to another child or parent on my watch again. I love the district that I work in and I do not want to shed any negative on it at all. I am very proud to work for it and there are so many positives, but I need to share my son's story, and this is some of what happened.

We helped Cody buy a truck when he turned sixteen and he wanted to turn it in for a car. Of course, we helped him do all of this. We were both guilty of giving our kids what they wanted. We both worked hard and expected things from our kids as well, but I will admit when it came to Cody, we often bailed him out, which I'm sure looking back on it made him less resilient and able to handle his own problems. So, yes, we are guilty of having high expectations, but giving in and helping too much with Cody. He did not have a good driving record; he had hit a mailbox and had a couple of tickets.

Well, you can imagine with school being a struggle and not being able to read or write well, what does a struggling student do? Sluff. And so, he did. I would get the phone calls and there would be questions, lies, consequences. This continued on, but being a teacher, I was not going to let him fail. We battled all of the time. I would check on his missing work. We would sit down and do it and as graduation came closer and he had classes to make-up, packets to do, and money to be paid before he would be allowed to receive his diploma. Thank goodness for his high school counselor at Stansbury High School his senior year, or he may not have graduated. She was very helpful, and I certainly had a role in it too. Yes, I am taking some credit. It was a daily battle. By the time he graduated, I felt like I was graduating too.

It upsets me, however, that during that time some red flags came up the summer before his senior year and a couple of incidents just a month before graduation that in my opinion, were very crucial events that could have made a big impact on the next seven years: some of the school personnel did not handle situations professionally nor with the student (Cody) in mind, we as parents thought we were doing all that we could - but we failed as well, the way the justice system handles drug arrests may be flawed, Cody again met the wrong people, and Cody failed himself. Here are some of those events...

His relationship with his girlfriend at the time was up and down. Neither of them are to blame, it was just young love. It was his first love and they had been going out since sophomore year of high school. They were a lot alike with some similar personality traits. They would be inseparable and then break-up. He would get very depressed. He would talk about suicide and we took him into the hospital. I had also taken him to the doctor and he was prescribed anti-depressants.

In March of 2009, we moved across Stansbury Park to a new house. It was a lot bigger. Everyone had more space and everything was a lot nicer. We had lived in the other house for twenty-five years. It was our first house after we got married. The kids had grown-up there and they were sad for about a week. We were all happy. Things were going really well for quite a while. However, looking back, in our other house, which was smaller it had been easier to keep a closer eye on Cody. His bedroom was right next to ours. We didn't have a basement so, we watched TV together more. That house was 16,00 sq. ft. versus the new house being 3,200 sq. ft. His room was in the basement and ours was upstairs. It was easier to come and go and become more distant. So, even though we were happy, he was older and becoming more independent, which was fine except he began to have more secrets. When we started to suspect things with a bigger house came more places to hide things and more ways to sneak things in or out.

In about April 2010, the assistant principal called me and said that Cody had looked up how to grow marijuana on the computer. A meeting was set up to talk about this behavior and I asked for the counselor to also be there to talk about graduation as well to see if everything was in order. I was under the impression that we would be meeting with the assistant principal and the counselor. Duane, Cody, and I showed up and had to wait for about 30 minutes and when we went into the office we were met by the other assistant principal, the principal, and the school resource officer as well as the assistant principal I spoke with on the phone with and the counselor. We felt like we were being ambushed. We were prepared to have Cody face the consequences the loss of computer use according to the policy. There wasn't any mention of the misuse of the computer or of his academics for graduation or how to help him. The meeting consisted of one of the assistant principals trying to get Cody's cell phone away from him and telling us that the drug task force was looking into him. A few days after that, the same assistant principal called in Cody's girlfriend and her mom. Then the mom called me and told me that he had told them not to hang around Cody because he was a bad kid. I did not say anything to Cody, but his girlfriend did and Cody came to me sobbing not wanting to go ever back to school. It was genuine not a ploy to not go to school. He sincerely felt like no one liked him and they were "out to get him."

A week or two later, Cody was arrested coming back from Salt Lake. He was pulled over by an undercover police officer. He and his friend had marijuana and paraphernalia in the car. He went to jail and a coach, who also worked at the jail, told the whole school. I'm sure that word may have gotten out anyway, but as a school employee that should be there for every student in my opinion, I don't understand why he felt the need to do that. It was hurtful to Cody. We hired an attorney for $10,000, which was the beginning (little did we know then), of many years of not only financial bailouts, but medical and emotional. Since Cody was 18, he went to an adult jail. When your child calls you from jail, it rips your heart out. When you see your child behind the glass in a jail, (yes, he was 18, but still a child in high school, yes, he should have known better, I'm not making excuses, I'm just stating how a mother feels) it rips your heart out. When you think about your child being in a cold jail cell alone, you can't sleep at night imagining the worst things that can happen to him. When you see your child enter a courtroom in an orange jumpsuit and shackles and try to keep a straight face for him, it tears you up inside. He broke the law and yes, I understand that he needed to face the consequences, but it is still heartbreaking for a parent. It's a feeling that never goes away. The thought of it still makes me nauseated to this day.

He took a plea of obeyance and was able to graduate. We talked about his second chance and making things right. He had been very scared and seemed genuinely determined to make things right in his life.

The next week Duane, Kaylee, and Cody went to Tooele for something and they had Cody be the one to call me to ask if he could bring a dog home from a mobile animal shelter that was set-up in the parking lot of Cal Ranch. I said no, but he said he felt sorry for her because it was like she was in dog jail, nobody cared about her and she needed a home. Well, I caved and they brought home a chocolate lab mix that we named Avery. Besides chewing up Kaylee's carpet and the carpet in a hotel room due to her anxiety (how ironic since Cody had major anxiety), she has been the best dog that we have ever had. This is also when he got his tattoo, "Life Rolls On," across his chest above his heart. He told me that bad things can happen, but you need to keep on going and make the best of it.

The part that came next was drug court. Here's how that works...you are assigned a color; you call in every day at like 7 AM and listen for your color. If your color is called you need to go into AP & P (Adult Probation and Parole) to have a urine test at a time they say. I'm not saying I agree or disagree with the program. I'm not sure what the success rate is. I've known some that this has been very successful for and some not. I just know they make it hard if you have a job and no transportation. We had hoped that this would work for Cody and that he had been scared and these restrictions would help get him on the right track. All of these people have lost their driver's licenses so, they have to get there by a certain time and if they have a job, which is one of the requirements of the probation, hopefully, their employer will work with them. This may have been us enabling Cody again, but we wanted to make sure that he made it to the urine test, court, group sessions, and a job so, since he didn't have a license, we gave him a ride. It was not easy. The times of these things were all over the place and unpredictable. I guess we could have made him ride a bike or walk. Most of those things were all approximately ten miles away. There were many fines and all of the urine tests, and group sessions had a fee. At first, he didn't have a job so, we paid until he could. This went on for a year and he graduated from drug court.

During that year, I had finished my master's degree in administration and was offered a job as an assistant principal at a high-school. I was nervous a little bit because all of my experience had been in elementary school. However, the superintendent at that time was amazing and she had complete confidence in me. I went into the job ready to make a difference. I found out very quickly that secondary students have the same needs as elementary students. They need someone to care. I was able to use my philosophy of building relationships and respect first, then figuring out their academics to help many students succeed. I made it a point to get to know every student. I would greet them at the door in the morning. If they weren't in class, I would chase them down and find out why. If they were failing, I found out why. I also went to all of their activities so they knew that I cared. I made sure that they graduated. I think my experiences with Cody helped me make a difference. I wished I could have made a difference with him sooner. I had a ten minute commute each day to work and I would pray each day, "Thank you God for giving me this opportunity to help these kids now, let me help my own." I was in secondary for two years and it is a rewarding job where you can make a difference, but when the opportunity came to move to an elementary school as a principal, I took it. I have been in that position for seven years, but strangely enough as I am nearing retirement or maybe as I'm writing this book stirring up all of these memories, I am considering going back to a secondary school.

We had our ups and downs for a few years. Things were going along quite well for us as a family. Cody worked a few different jobs and was supporting himself, however both Cody and Kaylee still lived with us, but we did not mind that as long as they were working. Having your adult children around and having a good relationship with them is the best. I only wish that relationship and those good times could have lasted forever with them both.

The following spring and summer of 2014, things started to change. Some of Cody's friends started to not hang around him. He was getting skinny. He was sick a lot. He was pawning things. Kaylee went with him somewhere and later said that she noticed that he was snorting pills. He wasn't prescribed opioids, but he graduated to them from new friends that he hung around. I believe it was oxycodone and eventually Xanax along with other benzodiazepines. (I later found out that he would sell or trade his pills and pot for them.) He ended up quitting two jobs in a row, getting a couple of speeding tickets and rear-ending two people within the year. He was back to living in hell again. We all were. He also had to go to court for theft. He walked out of a store in Salt Lake with a candy bar in his back pocket. He told me that he was not stealing it. I did totally believe him when he said that was not stealing it and that he was carrying it through the store, stopped to look at something and stuck it in his back pocket with it hanging out and totally forgot about it because that was typical Cody. He was always losing everything. Regardless, he had to go before a judge and pay a fine and the judge said that he could later get it taken off his record, but that would take a while and would come back to haunt him in the future when applying for jobs.

We did our own family interventions and he turn things around. After that, things went well for quite a while again. He had a job that he loved. He was back hunting and fishing with his friends. Then I would smell weed on him. That was a constant battle. In today's society, there are so many differences in opinion like: Is it a big deal or not? Is it the gateway drug? Can it help with a, b, or c? There are so many medicinal claims that it helps with this or that. Is it legal in this state or that state? To be honest, I'm not sure what my opinion is. I've read research about it either way. Cody's opinion was, however, that it helped him and he was never going to stop doing it. So, it was a constant argument because Duane and I are definitely law-abiding citizens and it is not legal in Utah. We were clear to Cody that it would not be used or brought into our house. I had to live in constant fear, however, of him being caught with it and going to jail, driving with it or under the influence of it, the police raiding our house and me losing my job because he might have it hid in the basement. It was an ongoing battle. Things were rough again for a while. His relationship with his girlfriend was up and down again. I want to be clear that I am still in contact with her today and she is great. It was just that they were young and immature. In fact, I have gotten along with all of his girlfriends and am still in contact with some of them. I know that being with Cody and his ups and downs was not easy. Duane and I always wished that he would have gotten married, had a child and maybe that would have made a difference and kept him from relapsing so many times, perhaps saving his life. He would have been a great dad. He loved kids. However, I wouldn't have wanted any woman as his wife to go through living a life with a husband that wasn't sober and I certainly wouldn't have wanted a grandchild to have a father suffering from addiction or worse yet to be without a father.

In the fall of 2015, I suspected that Cody was back using pot again. Then I started to find pieces of foil around his room. I did not know what that was. He got pulled over by a police officer that was always watching him, following him for no reason, it was almost like she would target him. She said that he crossed the yellow line (he does that often looking for deer or ducks). He swore that he had not been using anything. However, he was charged with a DUI even though he passed a series of all of the sobriety tests. They did a blood test before he had called me and I got there and it had shown a trace of marijuana in his system that could have been from long ago since it stays in your system for thirty days according to the lawyer. We got a lawyer for $5,000 and the case was pleaded down. The law stated that if there is even a trace of marijuana in his system then he can be charged even if it wasn't from that day. He lost his license for three months.

Then our worst fear ever came true, we found out that he had succumbed to the peer pressure of his new "so-called friends" and tried heroin. We wanted to get him help. Duane was willing to sell everything we owned to pay for rehab. I started to look into things and called places and insurance. This is an absolute joke. It is so hard to get help! At least it was for us, maybe because we didn't know what we were doing, or who or where to turn to. We would get things like our insurance wouldn't pay for inpatient treatment, unless certain steps were followed first.

Here's what had to be done after many calls around, a long drive and full day of waiting at one hospital only to be turned away. On another occasion, we drove to Ogden, Utah where they had him fill out paperwork for an evaluation, which took a couple of hours. Then we were turned away and not admitted. As part of the process, you had to be admitted to a detox place in the hospital first, but the only way to be admitted into detox was that you pretty much had to be high. Yes, that's right you had to be on something when you went in so, we went in the next day to LDS hospital in Salt Lake City, I didn't ask and Cody didn't tell until we got in the ER and were talking to the doctor about what he had used and what he had used in the past. Wow, for a mother who thought she knew a lot about her children and the world, I was dumb. I listened as he told the doctor about everything that he had used and for how long. We sat there for a few hours and I just prayed over and over that he would be admitted and get the help that he needed. He was admitted. He stayed for three days. We wanted him to go to outpatient care and he was willing, but then when he was home, he wouldn't go. We tried, but again he was an adult. Detox lasts between 3 to 5 days and is the first step in rehabilitation. The next step is an outpatient program. He wanted to do it on his own. He said that he already knew about the 12 step program from drug court and the group counseling so, he was sure that he could do it on his own. He was confident that he would do well this time. He cut himself off from the new friends that were bad influences, he stayed home, he got a job, and a new cell phone number (we did this two or three times over the years) so, that only the people that he wanted, who were positive influences in his life could get ahold of him. He did well for quite a while.

We even talked about having Cody go to live with relatives out of state so, he would not be tempted to go back to old habits and routines. We kept him busy. We did a lot of things together. Duane helped him look for jobs that he would like in other nearby states. He stayed away from bad influences.

Then he called me one day begging for help. He had relapsed and wanted to go to a doctor to try a medication that was supposed to help called suboxone. Well, when suboxone first came out it was very expensive and not covered by insurance. There were also very few doctors that were available to prescribe it that were covered on our insurance. It is a controlled substance so; the patient needs to go to the doctor monthly to have a written prescription and to have bloodwork and counseling (not sure how effective that is/was). So, I called around for a whole day and found a doctor in Bountiful, Utah. There was an initial down payment of $400 and then it was $400 a month. They gave us a discount card for the first month. I put it on my credit card. This worked for quite a while. Here's just a little bit of information about suboxone: It comes in a pill or a film that you put under your tongue to let it dissolve. It contains buprenorphine, which is an opioid medication/narcotic and naloxone, which blocks the effects of opioid medication such as the feelings of pain relief and well-being that lead to opioid abuse. The warnings on suboxone say that it can slow your breathing and may be habit-forming. Some of the common side effects include: constipation, diarrhea, headache, nausea, chills, fever, dizziness, flushed skin, sweating, painful urination, back or side pain, and insomnia. I read in one article that long term use may cause infertility. Duane was not in favor of this. He is like me and he did his own research and to him, it sounded like just another thing to become addicted to. Looking at it now, I tend to agree somewhat, as he mentioned to me, it seems like the people who are prescribed it will always be on it. It has come down in price. It did help Cody for a while. I do know other people that have been prescribed suboxone and it has worked for them for years. What about the people that don't have insurance though? Wow!

As I said, this worked for a while, but we did switch doctors twice and somewhere along the way one of them prescribed Cody, Klonopin (Clonazepam) for anxiety. A few of the many side effects include: difficulty breathing, dizziness, feeling sad, headache, irritability, lack of appetite shakiness, drowsiness, trouble sleeping, and more.

Wow. I know what you are thinking. I am thinking the same thing, what kind of mother lets their child take these medications. It was not until this moment right now, as I am researching for this book, looking up all of the side effects of these various drugs and actually piecing a timeline together that I am now realizing what a complete failure I was as a parent. I totally failed my son. Thinking back on it now, I should have been more proactive and said, NO, to another prescription! I do remember questioning Cody about it. I remember him getting angry and telling me that it was what the doctor said would help him. I did ask at the third doctor to have my name put on the release of information form, but by that time Cody was 24 and he didn't want me in his business. He could handle it. I also found out that sometimes when patients are admitted to detox in the hospital, they are given different types of medications to help them. Cody suffered from severe leg pains and was given Gabapentin, which many claim isn't addictive. This is just my own opinion, but I am predicting that our next drug crisis will stem from either Gabapentin or benzos. Yes, I will beat myself up forever about the prescriptions that my son was given and what I should have done to speak up or help control them, but there is also some part of me that trusted in the doctors that prescribed them.

I recently read an article that was shared by someone on my Facebook page talking about if a person has depression and anxiety, it's like having a brain that is at war with itself. Having both of these types of mental illness is a real challenge. Anxiety is having an overactive mind where your thoughts are always racing telling you that you need to do this, or you can't do that, which can be disorienting and frustrating. It was described as your brain being pushed against your skull making you want to scream. Depression is having an underactive mind. It's the voice in a person's head shouting to them that nothing they do matters and that they should just roll over and die. It's the guilt and the feeling of hopelessness weighing a person down so much so, that they are physically unable to get up and function. So, maybe medication is needed, but how effective is it and how do we monitor it well?

So, we continued on and had our ups and downs for a while. We had a lot of good times that I will treasure forever. I loved to see my son happy. He was a hard worker and did a great job. He wanted to please everyone. He loved it when he was told what a good job he was doing at work! He was so proud. He craved attention and loved to have fun. He enjoyed being with his dad hunting and fishing. There were a lot of times that he wouldn't go out to the movies or to eat with us. He later told me why when he started to hang out with us all of the time, he said that it was because he did not want to run into any of his old acquaintances that they were a bad influence on him. So, he was doing well, but as an addict, you are always an addict because the craving is always there. One little thing can trigger a relapse, or maybe there is no trigger, but just succumbing to the strong craving. If he was criticized at work, or something went wrong, which a lot of things went wrong for him on a daily basis either due to his previous drug use and its effects on his brain, ADHD, or just plain bad luck, which he had a lot of; he would turn to something to relieve the pain. Again, it is easy to blame myself. I should have taught him better coping skills and how to be more resilient. I should have helped him be more independent and not been so enabling? I wish that he would have come to me. He knew that he could! He did later on more and more. Why didn't he come to me every time that he needed help right from the beginning? What did I do wrong?

In the summer of 2016, Duane's dad hadn't been doing that great health-wise and had been wanting to go fishing. Duane had to work weekends so, Cody and I took Ron fishing to Flaming Gorge, the Gillette family's favorite place to fish in June. I was a little nervous because Ron's boat was big, but Cody wanted me to go and were all worried that Ron didn't have too many fishing trips left in him. So, off we went. Cody had been doing really well. He had been trying hard. While we were there, he was sick most of the time with many of the symptoms that I had mentioned before. I took care of him, but it was hard. He was nauseated, had diarrhea, aches, and pains. He was tired and weak. When he did sleep, we slept down below in sleeping bags. His phone went off constantly all night long. Even though it was on silent, it woke me up as I am a light sleeper so, curious and being his mother, I reached for it. There were people bugging him all hours of the night wanting to trade for this and that. There were many times I wondered if I should call the police and turn everyone in. I didn't. Right or wrong. I don't know. Again, you may be judging me, but you were not in my situation. I knew parents that had turned their own children in to the police and their children had turned their lives around. I also knew of addicts that have been in and out of jail and their lives are forever ruined unable to find a job, unable to drive, vote, own a gun (for Cody this would mean not ever hunting again), with multiple felonies. Some may say, they are breaking the law and that is what they deserve. I'm not sure what the right answer is. I'm not sure that messages on a phone are even enough evidence. They sure weren't later when it came to prosecute the people involved in the death of my son.

We all went to Flaming Gorge again with Duane in July. Cody was still trying and taking his suboxone. He was tired and irritable, which sometimes causes Duane and him to clash so, it was an okay weekend, but not the best. Cody was still trying though. It was good that we went because that was the last fishing trip that Ron went on. He passed away in July of 2017.

Here's the thing about addiction, many people say that it's a matter of choice. Yes, it is. In the beginning, that first time the addict tries the drug either because of peer pressure, other outside pressure, some type of mental illness like depression, just for fun, or whatever the reason it is ultimately their choice. However, from that time on the brain is changed. The pleasure centers/sensors in the brain are changed and the slide down the slippery slope begins.

So, when the bad times came, as we like to refer to them as World War ??? (we lost track of what number we were on). There were very awful, rotten things said. We were all hurt. I always quickly forgave Cody. I knew it wasn't him talking and that it was the drugs. In fact, he would get mad, yell, break, punch, and destroy things for about 30 minutes then he would break down crying for 30 minutes. The next day he wouldn't even remember what had happened.

We went on a trip for spring break to Lake Powell in the spring of 2017, and it was pure hell. Then the next few months things got worse. Cody asked to go to rehab again. I called around and really wanted to get him in an inhouse rehab this time. When I say that I called around, I mean I called all over the state trying to find a place that had openings, would take our insurance, take payments, which were like 80-20% after deductible was met. I was trying to find one that wasn't $100,000, or didn't have a wait list since he was asking and wanting to go. I finally had a guy in St. George call me back. Here's the thing about inpatient treatment centers, which I couldn't believe at first, until I verified it with my insurance and the hospital as well, in order to qualify you need to of had three unsuccessful visits to rehabs first. What? Really? Okay, let that sink in a minute...yes, that's right you can't just get into an inpatient rehab until you've tried three other types of rehab first like, detox and outpatient and failed three times then you can qualify. So, again, I turned a blind eye as Cody did what he needed to do in order for us to go to the hospital ER and have him admitted into detox. Again, I was on pins and needles waiting and praying that they would admit him. They did. He stayed the three days and this time was all lined up to go to the outpatient day treatment. However, when it came right down to it, he didn't go.

There were a few times that Cody had asked me about trying some other medications that he had researched or heard about. One of them was Subutex, which is also known as Buprenorphine. It can be more habit forming that Suboxone so, I was glad when our insurance did not cover it. Another one was Vivitrol, which is an injection mainly used to prevent relapse in people that have become dependent on opioids and heroin then stopped using them. It is supposed to keep them from feeling the need or craving to use the drug. I read about it and it sounded like a good idea. However, it was not covered by our insurance and the cost was high. It was about $1500 per shot and the shots were needed once a month. Looking back on this, I wish that we would have tried it. Now, I would pay any amount of money to have my son back. I have recently read a book titled, "Everything is Horrible and Wonderful," however, about Harris Whittels written by his sister,

Stephanie and she talked about his addiction to heroin and his death. He had been in and out of several rehabs and he had tried the Vivitrol shot, but it hadn't worked so, I don't know why some addicts are able to recover and beat their addiction, while some relapse time after time and either live a life of pain and sorrow or die.

One other thing Cody wanted to try was a methadone clinic. They have one in Salt Lake, a person struggling with an opioid addiction can walk into a methadone clinic and request to be treated. There is an interview/exam and patients can receive methadone on-site. The clinics are regulated by the state and the medication is dispensed by a licensed practitioner, who can give out opioids. Duane was very much against this and I agreed. Methadone, from what we read was highly addictive itself and you had to go to the clinic quite often. It can be daily in some cases and a person my need the treatment for a long time. It did not seem like the right solution.

When I had been calling around for inpatient treatment centers, one of the places had gotten my name and they called me back a month later. They didn't have a room, but they put me in contact with a place in Michigan. I was in contact with them back and forth for a week. They have grants that will pay for what your insurance doesn't pay for. They would send a person out and do an intervention type thing to convince Cody to go. I told Duane and Kaylee about it. Kaylee thought it was a good idea, but Duane didn't. I eventually got Duane to speak with them on the phone. We told Cody about it because I believe in honesty. He did not want to go. He did not want to leave the state and go that far away. Maybe I should have pushed this more, but there were some red flags in the back of my mind about it seeming too good to be true because they were very persistent (no other places are that way it's all on you) and basically free. However, it really got him thinking and wanting to try to be "clean."

He went for four months doing really well though. He was even telling me what he and his doctor were talking about. The doctor called and spoke with me on the phone. In fact, he said that the doctor had suggested that he give his suboxone and other pills to me and that I monitor them. So, we did that for a while. I would set them out at the times of day when it was time to take them. At that time, we had my mom living with us because she had fallen and broken a bone in her back. He was helpful in taking care of her. He was even doing well despite the terrible incident of bad luck that happened in August. His key fob for his truck was not working so, we took it in and had it repaired at the local dealer. It was an electrical issue and they repaired the parts of a broken wire that ran along the bottom of the truck. A few weeks later, I was in a meeting and Cody called me saying his truck was on fire! Thank goodness he was able to pull over and get out without getting hurt. However, his truck was completely burnt up, along with a telephone pole, and part of another truck that was along the side of the road where he was forced to pull over. It was awful. He had a really special watch that his Grandpa Ron had given him in there and some other things that couldn't be replaced. He was patient and in okay spirits waiting for the insurance claim though. Interestingly enough, the fire started in the undercarriage of the truck and was electrical that had just been repaired. It was not Cody's fault rather bad luck.

Around this same time, he had met a girl with two kids and he brought her and the kids to our house. Duane and I loved them. Cody was great with them. I started to notice though that he was making trips to Salt Lake a lot. I didn't like that. I knew that he was using again and unfortunately their relationship didn't last probably because of his drug use, but I am still in contact with her today because she had two little boys that Cody adored. We loved to see them play together.

Then as the pattern goes, everything that goes up must come down. So, our good times were about to crash. And crash they did. Cody had a doctor's appointment in Salt Lake in October 2017, he must not of had enough gas in his truck (we had given him Duane's white truck to drive in the meantime waiting for the insurance claim) and was late so, he drove Duane's Porsche to his doctor's appointment. Around 4:30 PM, he called me very upset, he said that he had wrecked and that he was in dad's car. Now, over the years, I have received a handful of these calls, and I still regret to this day that once again, I am a bad parent because my first reaction wasn't are you okay, but more about what happened, what were you doing, and what is the damage? What the hell was wrong with me? Who cares? I do not give a crap about a car! I would give an infinite number of cars to have my son back, I hope that he knows that! This time however, the first thing that I asked was if he was okay. He said that he was, but that his back hurt a little. I told him that I was on my way and I would be there right away. He said that the police were just showing up.

Duane and I were both on the phone with him back and forth. The place that he had wrecked was on the really busy off-ramp coming from Salt Lake on I-80 exiting to Tooele. He had hit the side cement barrier at a high speed. He doesn't remember. He was quite shaken. Duane had gotten there just before me. The highway patrol officer had given him a sobriety test and the ambulance was taking him to the hospital so we followed it. The car didn't look too bad to me, but the frame was bent so, it ended up being totaled. At the hospital, they found him to have a slight concussion and bruised ribs. Thank God he was okay. The only substances in his system were his prescription medications and they were at not above the levels that they shouldn't have been, but he had not passed the field sobriety test so, he was charged with a DUI and they took him to jail.

Later when he called, asking for us to come and get him. I wanted to leave him there. I don't know why this time I felt he needed to stay even though it seemed that it was an accident. I guess it was that we were out of money. How much more can we spend? We could not afford a lawyer this time. Maybe it was because I was just tired. How much more could we take? Maybe it was because I was really scared. Deep down I had always thought about the possibilities of the outcome of Cody's life being one of these: Possibility number one...he would finally get the help he needed, get a good job that he liked, marry a great wife and be in love, have children and be an awesome dad. Number two, he would end up in jail or prison. Number three, he would continue on with the struggling life of addiction forever. Number four, God forbid, he would accidentally hurt somebody or himself.

Fortunately, or unfortunately, Duane and I were never on the same page at the same time. When one of us was exhausted and had enough the other was able to calmly function and deal with things. Cody called over and over nonstop wanting us to bail him out. I was staying strong because I thought that is what Duane wanted, he is the one that said to call the bail bondsman and bail him out. So, that is what we did. Looking back on that now, I do feel that it was the right decision.

When Cody went to court, he was given a public defender. He was not very good. In fact, I do not think he did anything at all to help Cody. In some ways, that's okay because even though we are a local town and my family and I know that judge, there was no favoritism. He was hard on Cody. He was doing it in a kind way to make sure that this was it and it was seriously time to get his act together. We watched a few cases before his and they weren't given as tough of stipulations as Cody. He was ordered on house arrest for a month, of course fines, the loss of his license, ordered to attend scheduled court dates, he had to do weekly check-ins with a probation officer, and was allowed to do community service to help pay off some of the fines. The judge knew me and he made it clear to Cody that he was to pay the fines on his own and not have us do it.

Cody was very much impacted by this. House arrest pretty much sucked as it should. There was a lot of time to reflect on things and it was very boring for him. I was worried about him getting depressed. It was during this time that we really grew closer than we have ever been.

Even though I would come home from work exhausted, I would stay up late with him talking and watching movies on Netflix. I knew that he had been home alone bored all day. Plus, he was opening up to me and talking to me about everything. We became the best of friends. I was able to give him great advice with him being completely sober and really attentive. He was setting goals and really listening. There was real hope for the future.

About a month later, the medical bills came rolling in from the accident. The hospital had charged him outrageous costs. Instead of charging for one MRI they charged the MRIs separately one charge for the head, one for the back and one for the ribs. The insurance was refusing to pay because he was being charged with a DUI. Next, came a letter from Allstate and they were dropping us after 30 years for too many claims. In a few months, Cody was going to be 26 and would need to find his own medical insurance in order to keep seeing his doctor and keep his prescriptions. He was in a deep, deep hole and I didn't know how he was going to get out of it, but we wouldn't give up.

He started his community service at the garbage dump. He mostly stayed home with us and did things with us. Our relationships were good. He had a great birthday in December. We had the best Christmas ever with not many gifts, but a lot of laughs and family time. Duane's mom stayed with us.

He met a new girl in January and that seemed to go well for a while, but then an old friend came back into the picture and it was not good. I watched him close, however and all of us were always searching his room. In fact, he called me once in February and asked me to come and get him from a friend's house because there were people doing drugs there and he didn't want to be around it.

He stayed strong. Not perfect, but strong. He stayed on the path toward his goals. He went to court in March and had a good review, he was planning on starting a really good job in a week that he was super excited about, and was thrilled to be going to the Jazz game with my brother Aaron, and then March 1, 2018, everything shattered.

Chapter 9

Shattered

"Tears are words that need to be written."

~ Paulo Coelho

March 1, 2018, will forever be the worst day of our lives. I know that I speak for myself as well as both Duane and Kaylee. Nothing will ever be the same again.

I want to start just a few days before that on Sunday, Cody hadn't been feeling well for the past week and on that day, he had a fever. He was very achy and complaining of a sore throat. I took him into the clinic in Tooele. I knew that he definitely wasn't feeling well at all because it is always at least an hour wait there and I dreaded going there with him because he never had the patience to wait that long and would be really restless, but this time he just sat there really lethargic. Now, I'm not a doctor, but I am a mom, and there have been many times when my "Cody radar" as I call it has been right. We have been sent home from the doctor's office even after me telling them that there was something really wrong with him and sure enough, we would end up coming back a few days later with a very serious sickness like pneumonia and the swine flu. I knew this kid and my intuition was strong when it came to something not being right with him. He had always been my sickly child. I was certain this time that it was strep. He could hardly swallow. Well, three and a half hours later (I am not exaggerating) with tests and all they sent us home saying it was just a virus? What? So, I went to Walmart and bought some over the counter medication, chicken noodle soup, Gatorade, and we went home. He laid on the couch and we watched Netflix while I tickled his face and took care of him.

Monday morning, I had taken off work because he had court. It went really well. He had been doing everything that had been required from the charges he had received in the fall. We went back home, I made him soup, he watched TV resting on the couch while I did some work from home at the kitchen table.

I remember us talking about how things were looking up for him. I told him that I was proud of him for how well he was doing. I told him that he could do it! He was really excited about starting a new job in a few days that paid well and that he knew and liked the people he would be working with. He said it was a job that he could see doing long term. He was also really excited about going to the Jazz game on Friday with my brother, Aaron, who had gotten them really great tickets.

On Tuesday, I went to work and then after work I went to my STEM endorsement class.

Our class got our early so, I remember getting home and sitting at the dinner table around 7 o'clock and looking into Cody's eyes and I could tell that he was high. It bothered me. I was angry. It wasn't heroin. I'm not sure what. I didn't say anything. I just gave him a look of disappointment. I should have said something. I don't know why I didn't, maybe I was in shock because he had been doing so well, too tired to fight, too sad to face it, I don't know? He laid on the couch still not feeling better and we watched TV until everyone went to bed.

On Wednesday, I went to work. Cody called me between 10 and 11 AM. He said that he was feeling a little better. He asked what time I would be home like he always did. I told him that I had a meeting and that I would be home around 5:00 so, his dad would give him a ride to group (as part of his court obligation he was attending group counseling at Aspen Ridge). He really liked his counselor. He told me that group was cancelled. I thought that was strange for maybe a second so, I asked a bit more about it and he told me that it was because too many people were also sick.

I later found out that this was not true and that he had called in sick to group. I don't know why...I can only assume that maybe he was a little anxious about starting a new job and like most addicts, they have that strong craving to just "take one last hit" before quitting for good and leaving that life behind them to move on for good to a better life. I don't know why?

While the events and feelings of that night are still crystal clear and will forever be etched in our minds, there are some things that just do not make any sense. I truly believe that there was a higher power at work that night and that some things are meant to be for a reason. There were so many things/feelings that happened that were out of character for me. My intuition/Cody radar was telling me to do one thing, but something else in my mind was telling me not to.

So, at the risk of sounding a bit out there, I will continue to tell the story of the worst night of our lives. I'm going to let you know a history of how things usually run in our household. From the time Cody was little (it's part of our bond), he always needed to know where I was. (Now, that my dad lives with me, he has taken over Cody's role, but that's a different story.) Anyway, him calling me and asking when I will be home was a regular occurrence. I think it made him feel safe and relieved his anxiety. When he called earlier in the day and asked when I would be home and I said around 5:00, normally he would be calling when it got closer to 5:00 if I wasn't home, but he didn't, and I didn't call before I left like I usually do. Also, after his explanation about group being canceled, I didn't think anything more of it, which, normally I probably would have called to verify that. I had no bad feelings on my Cody radar that day. As I mentioned before, I had this thing, intuition I guess, being a mom, that unbreakable bond, that I always got a feeling when something was right, or especially when something was not right, or about to happen with Cody. Duane can confirm that it's true. I can sense things. I later found out I'm what some say an empath.

When I got home, Duane was making dinner and it was about ready- he is amazing like that. It was a family favorite, beef noodles which, I can no longer stand the smell of let alone eat and I didn't realize it until quite a while later when I started writing this book, that my brain must associate it with that night and it makes me sick to my stomach. Duane will normally text Cody when he is downstairs in his room to tell him that dinner is ready, and I will also call over the railing at the stairs for him to come up. Kaylee wasn't home from work yet. Cody didn't respond to Duane's text. So, I said that I would go down and get him, but Duane said that he thought he had heard him leave once out the front door and wasn't sure if he came back in or not, but that he had also said earlier that he still didn't feel well and was going to sleep. So, I said okay, and I didn't go down to his room. This was very out of character for me! Normally, I would go down there, knock on his door, check anyway, ask how he was doing, and bring him food if he didn't feel well. What was wrong with me? Why did I not do those things? It's so weird, but something was telling me... No, just let him sleep.

Then a few hours later I was like, "Are you sure he came back in and is even down there?" So, Duane used the Find My Friends App and it showed that he was home. So, again I thought I should go check on him, but something told me No, let him sleep. This was extremely out of character for me. Even for Duane, it was strange behavior by now to not go check on him. Seriously, you're probably thinking what kind of parents are they? A year later, yes, that's how long it took for Duane to share his guilt, he shared with me that something also kept him from going down to check on Cody as well. He said that he felt that something was wrong and was afraid to go down there. Oh, how I wish he would have disclosed that sooner. He held that in for a long time and I'm sure he won't appreciate me sharing it with the world now, but men grieve so differently than women. Not just that, all people grieve differently, and I want to not only celebrate my son by writing this book, but hopefully help even just one person. I think he thought that I would blame him. I don't! I could blame myself. I don't. It was God's plan. We did not go down there because it was Cody's time to go to be with Him.

Again, at about 9:30 just before we went to bed, I thought to myself, I better go see how Cody is doing. Did I? No. Why? I don't know. We took Avery, the dog in our room with us and Kaylee opened our bedroom door at 10:30 to get her to take her down with her where she sleeps. It woke me up and I thought about going down to check on Cody then, but tossed and turned for three more hours instead.

Meanwhile, as Kaylee went downstairs, she stopped at Cody's door and put her hand on the doorknob to open his door and talk to him for a few minutes like she often did, but something stopped her. She said it was quiet which was odd because Cody was never quiet. She had a feeling to just go in her room and go to bed.

I woke up at 1:30 and finally said to myself, "What is wrong with you! Go check on Cody now!"

I went down the stairs and as I approached his room, his door was shut, but I could see that his light was on from the glow below the door. I gently knocked and quietly called out, "Hey Code," and I opened his door. As I opened the door, I saw him on the floor on his knees face down. I immediately yelled his name as I ran to him and dove on the floor beside him. I screamed, "No!" " Duane, Duane." Kaylee came running out of her room, I think she screamed. I yelled for someone to call 911 and got up meeting Duane at the stairs. Kaylee handed me the phone with the 911 operator on the line. I was back by Cody's side. I was focused. I looked at him. I rolled him slightly to his side hugging him. He was stiff. He stayed in a fetal position. How ironic. My baby boy. My precious baby boy. Gone. I knew it was too late. I calmly spoke with the operator because that's how I am in emergencies. I gave her the information on name, address, and all of that. She kept asking about

CPR. She didn't get it. I did. It was too late. Bless her. I told her. He isn't

breathing. No, it's too late for CPR. He's a little stiff. He's blue. He was

cold.

I handed the phone to Kaylee and laid by my son hugging him.

Why hadn't I checked on him sooner? Why? I remember yelling out that

I wanted the people responsible for giving him the drugs arrested. I laid

there with him. Then I glanced around the room. His room had been

spotless the day before. I had checked it because I was concerned about

him slipping and I always did frequent checks that becomes the normal

routine when you live with an addict. Plus, Kaylee had just cleaned the

whole basement and his room spotless on Sunday. His room wasn't

spotless now, there were pills scattered all over his dresser. I believe I

saw baggies of pot on his bed and marijuana was in the police report.

Then I saw a spoon next to a needle/syringe on the dresser and another

one on the floor full of a brownish liquid.

The police came quickly. I was stiff laying by my son's stiff body.

There was a small pool of blood on the floor. I think it came from his

nose due to his head being down. When the first officer came in. I got

up to talk to him and I was asked to leave and never allowed back in.

At the time I felt like they were invading our home. Even though they were polite and understanding, one after another they came in down to the basement. I can't even imagine doing their job seeing people die from overdoses day after day and the trauma it causes a family. I know that they were just doing their job and that this was now a crime scene, but wow that door was shut, and they were not letting me back in near my son period. They kept coming, detectives, the medical examiner, sheriffs, and someone from the drug task force. One of the detectives was very kind and empathetic. We answered all of his questions and he answered ours. They took pictures and bagged evidence. We showed them our Vivint camera recordings. We gave them some leads from his phone too as to who may have sold him the drugs. Later on, we came to the conclusion with our own investigating and are certain who did so. We have the proof.

It was surreal. At one point, as I was sitting there taking it all in and thinking about what I saw in Cody's room, I remember asking if we were in trouble or going to be arrested. The detective said no, absolutely not that Cody was an adult and it was clear that everything was his. We talked about how Cody had been doing so well and hadn't been using heroin that we knew of. He mentioned that is how a lot of overdoses happen. The person quits and then relapses. They think that they can use the same amount and it's too much. Again, I'm sure that the job of dealing with these situations is very hard. He left his contact information for us and told us what our next steps would be as far as contacting the funeral home, getting the police report, and the autopsy report from the state medical examiner.

We had been talking up in the kitchen and family room upstairs, I asked to go down to see my son before they took him, but I wasn't allowed to. It had been about three or four hours when they came up the stairs carrying Cody's body in a black body bag. That was a terrible sight as they carried him out the door and away. The door shut and there was silence.

It was 5:00 AM, Thursday, March 1, 2018, we just sat there in shock. Now what? I called my brother Aaron. His response was disbelief. I could tell that he was extremely upset and trying to hold himself together. He immediately came over. I called my brother Aric and he too was very upset. Then I called my administrative intern at that time and texted my director. We were supposed to have a faculty meeting that morning. They called me and they went forward with the meeting and made a plan of how to tell my staff and handle everything at my school. When it was a little bit later around 8:00 AM my brother went down to tell my dad in person and bring him over. He had been beginning to have signs of dementia so, I was worried about him being alone and how he would handle this. Around 10:00 AM both of my brothers and I went over to give our mom the news. I thought that she might totally lose it like she did when I had to tell her that her dad had passed away. Instead, she was upset, but not screaming and wailing like I thought she would. She wouldn't come over to my house with us though. She insisted on just staying at her house and being alone for a bit.

Duane and Kaylee had gone to get Duane's mom at the same time. As, I had mentioned before, she had just lost her husband the previous July and we were all worried about how she would take the news. I really think that Cody's death was just too much for his mom. She was doing okay. In fact, we had just had one of our best Christmases ever. There weren't a lot of gifts, but a lot of smiles and laughs. She would come on Sunday for dinner, but she quickly went downhill after this. She passed away in July of 2018, just four month later.

The rest of that day was filled with people coming by to pay their respects. Our close friends and one of the teachers from my school came over and totally took charge and helped. Our phones were immediately blowing up with calls, texts, and messages on social media with condolences. My Aunt Debbie and cousins Tishena, Sicily and her precious daughter Bailey were right on their way from South Dakota.

Through the next week, we had the most amazing support from family, friends, and community. We are truly blessed and surrounded by very kind and loving people. People came to visit and offer help and support. We had tons of food. We will forever be grateful to everyone. It made me realize just how important it is to do the same for others when they have a death in their family. Duane and I both agreed to be a lot better at supporting others like we were supported. Unfortunately, I have attended about eleven funerals in the last year. Hopefully, I've helped provide some comfort to the families.

On Friday, we began to plan a funeral. I had already helped with my grandma's and grandpa's funerals a little bit and recently done everything for Duane's dad's funeral so, I made my to do list then Duane, Kaylee, and I got started.

As we were sitting around that morning, just the three of us, we had one of our best, most honest conversations about it all. When you live with a family member with addiction it is like you are in an amusement park riding the rides only there's no amusement you are stuck on one ride over and over. We had been riding in on the "roller coaster through addiction hell" for years. Sometimes you are going slowly up, up, up the hill and things are fine, maybe even good, not scary, there's hope, but then you reach the top of the hill and you go downhill at a tremendous amount of speed. You are going so fast that you cannot control it like when a loved one is on a high, binge, or has a relapse. Then you go on some even twists and turns that aren't so bad. All of the sudden, however, there's the circle loop that turns you upside down. That's the point we were at. Our life had just been turned upside down in an instant. Then the ride coasts to an end. It's over and you have to get off. What do you do next? Some part of you always knew it would come to an end somehow some way.

That morning Duane was the most open and honest about his feelings than he had ever been. Like I said before, we are opposites and we were always opposites about how to handle the situations that arose during those dark years. In some ways that was a bad thing because we weren't a consistent team, but in other ways it was good because when one of us was literally at our wits-end and couldn't take it anymore the other was fine to step-up and handle things. It kept us together. It kept Cody in our home where we were able to try to help him. I know some parents may have kicked their children out. I am not going to give advice and I am certainly not going to judge other parents because I haven't walked a mile in their shoes. I only know that I lived with the fear that I may one day find my son dead and I did not want that to happen to him ever, but I definitely know that I could have never forgiven myself if it would have happened were he out homeless on the street somewhere. That's just me. I could not have kicked him out. I can live with knowing that I tried to help him. As Duane spoke, it was comforting to know that even though we had this horrific tragedy that we may never overcome, we had each other. When he hugged me, I thought to myself, we will all make it through this together. That only lasted a short while though. We had each other through the next few months, but then my dad's dementia got worse and I had to move him in, my mom wasn't doing well, and his mom soon died, He became withdrawn and doesn't talk about his feelings much. Like I said before, I know that everyone deals with grief in different ways that I realize. It makes it hard for a marriage to survive the loss of a child.

Kaylee is quieter like her dad. She talks to me a lot sometimes when we are alone however, that morning was a huge break-through. I'll admit I was kind of mad at her. In the last year, she pushed Cody away like most of the people in his life and that really bothered me. I get that she has a room in the basement that was next to Cody's and she saw and heard more than we knew. She dealt with a lot more. She is very black and white like her dad when it comes to drugs and addiction. To them, it was a question of, "Why doesn't he just stop?" It's that easy. For me, I understand, and I believe that it is a disease. I grew up with an alcoholic father and one brother (who is sober now and doing very well) that suffered from drug addiction. I have always believed that addiction is hereditary. I have watched my brother and Cody go through and down the same identical paths and for most of their lives they were never around each other.

Cody didn't remember or understand things he said or did to Kaylee when he was under the influence of drugs. His sister was his whole world and he loved her so much! So, when she would ignore him or do mean things like refuse to give him a ride to work or label the food in the pantry, he didn't understand and would call me crying. It broke my heart. It also hurt me to know that she was hurting really bad inside from seeing what he was doing to himself and our family. The names that he called her and me hurt. I could easily forgive and forget. It was harder for her.

As a mother who loved both of my children with my whole heart, it was always hard for them to understand my perspective and that I loved them both very, very much! They were jealous of each other and thought that I played favorites. Kaylee always thought that Cody was my favorite. That morning, I know she was filled with guilt like we all were. As we sat at the table looking at pictures to make a collage, we were finally able to talk about it all. I was able to tell her and help her understand that I loved them both very much! It was just that she was very independent, and that Cody needed me more. Through our tears, we came to all understand each other and we made our way to Tate Mortuary to meet with Cole Houghton.

I just couldn't get a clear picture in my mind of what Cody would want for his funeral. I kept searching my thoughts, but nothing was coming to me. I know that Duane and Kaylee wanted him to be cremated and that he would have wanted that as well, but I am more spiritual and traditional, and I wanted a casket. Then as we were sitting there making decisions, Kaylee saw an option where you could do both. It felt right and everything started to come together. The ideas were flowing. We found a guest book with a fish on it. An urn with a deer and a small little red heart urn on a stand. Kaylee ordered a softball necklace to put some of his ashes in and I found a heart for me. Duane already had a bullet key chain. We were able to use a casket for the funeral so; we chose a beautiful wooden one with white silk inlay.

What would we have him wear? Red was Cody's and my favorite color and of course camo for hunting. So, we would dress him in dress clothes and camo both because he liked fashion, in fact, we had just been talking about shopping; and camouflage for his love of hunting. We decided on a red shirt and tie with a camo button-down shirt left open and camo pants. It was decided that we would post all over Facebook and in the obituary for people to wear camo or red. It felt like we were honoring Cody and we were nailing it with all of his favorite things. He would have approved.

We went and picked out flowers, a wreath with red roses and

white lilies. Then a very cool casket spray with yellow sunflowers, and a mix of orange-red and purple wildflowers. We brought them some antlers to add to it. It was unique and totally him.

Then we went home and wrote the obituary, called my Pastor, worked on the collage and started on the program. What songs? Who would speak? Kaylee and I both decided that we would. As we worked on the program, other things came to mind like the reception after, food, and centerpieces. We rented the place across the street from the mortuary to have the reception. We chose Mexican food, which was one of Cody's favorites. He had told me recently that part of his five year plan was to go to Mexico with his friend Scott and meet his future wife. She would be an awesome cook he had said. Oh, how I wish I would have had the chance to see him married and be a grandma to "little Codys" running around. My friends, ladies from church and Beta sisters paid for the building and food as well as prepared it all. Again, something that we will forever be grateful for. Kaylee and her friends came over to make the centerpieces. They put camo duct tape around mason jars and filled them with cattails and then made camo and red ribbons for people to wear at the funeral. It was great to listen to them all together again talking like they used to, just too bad it was under horrific circumstances. Kaylee also worked on a video that turned out amazing.

Later Friday night, the mortuary called and let us know that Cody's body was being released from the state medical examiner's office in Salt Lake City and brought back to the mortuary in Tooele. We could meet them there. Duane and I drove in. He did not want to go in and see Cody like that. So, I went in and was led to the basement to a room where I saw my son's body lying on a cold steel table with a white sheet over him up to his neck.

They left me alone with him. I went to him and leaned over him and turned the sheet down a bit. His arms were crossed over his chest. I took one of his hands in mine and held it. I traced the other hand with my other hand. He was cold. I spoke to him. Honestly, I don't really remember what I said. I remember feeling peaceful though because I knew that yes, that was his body, but he was would now be in a better place. I remember telling him that I loved him. I stroked his cheek as I always did. His face...he was so very handsome. I wish in his life he would have known just how special he was and had a stronger self-esteem. He was handsome, smart, talented and vibrant. There were purple splotches on his face where the blood had settled because I had found him face down on his knees. I just stood there taking him in knowing this would be the last time I would see him and have time to him by myself. I wasn't creeped out and the image does not haunt me. It was more like a peaceful bonding. I asked God to please take care of my son.

I did become curious a bit because that is me, I always want to know the why and the facts. I had to know. Why had I not noticed? I looked at his arms to see if I could find needle marks. I didn't see any. I didn't look between his toes. Since then I've watched, read, and researched a lot about heroin and I know there are other places that users may inject themselves. I guess it doesn't' matter now.

I figured that I had been there a while and Duane was waiting in the car so, it was probably time to go. I kissed him on the cheek and turned to go. I walked toward the door. I couldn't leave. I went back. I stood and stared, memorizing every precious detail of him again. I did that about three more times. I ran back and held his hands in mine. I stared at those hands with the long skinny fingers. They felt rough and had dirt stains in between the cracks. I remembered how they used to shake when he was tying his lure on because he would get so excited. Finally, I took a deep breath and mustered up the courage to leave. First, I crossed his arms and peacefully placed them on his chest the way I found them. I glanced at his tattoo on the left side of his chest and read it...Life Rolls On. " God, please give me the strength for life to roll on," I whispered as I pulled the white sheet up to his neck, kissed him on the cheek, told him I loved him and that I would see him again. I turned and left.

It all came together. We were as ready as we could be. We went to bed almost a week later on Tuesday night feeling okay. I had gotten up that night after leaving the mortuary and started writing a speech for the funeral. My thoughts came pouring out and I had practiced reading it many times to everyone so, that I wouldn't cry. I know that Duane was very nervous. He kept asking if I was sure about doing it. He told me later that he thought for sure that he was going to have to go up and get me in the middle of it, but something happened Tuesday night that gave me the most amazing strength that I was able to honor my son with astounding poise and grace. I share this because it is one of the important events that has occurred in my life and I do not know how or why nor I can explain it, I can only say that it has played a major significance in my healing and outlook on life. Some people may believe me, and some may question me, but here is what I experienced. Duane, Kaylee and I went to bed that night before the funeral (I say Kaylee because for almost a month after Cody died she slept in our bedroom in our reclining chair – it was that hard on her) and at 1:30 a time that will haunt me forever, I woke up and I just looked around and didn't see anything. I heard Cody's voice very clearly say "mom" just how he always said it so, I opened my eyes and I didn't see anything. I closed my eyes again and his voice continued on. It/He said to me... "Mom, I'm okay. It was an accident. I didn't mean to do it. It had to be you that found me. It couldn't be dad and it couldn't be Kaylee. It had to be you, You are the strong one and you could handle it. I'm sorry. I love you." Then I started crying like the crying when, you are crying so hard that you are gasping and sucking in for air; and when I took a deep breath and went to exhale, I felt a coldness go from my inside my chest, through my whole body, down through my toes and out.

The next day we slowly and dreadfully got ready. As we arrived at the mortuary, neither Duane nor Kaylee wanted to go in to see Cody in the casket, but they did and after Duane told me that he was so glad that we had done both a casket and an urn because seeing Cody in the casket brought him some closure and peace. Cole and his staff had done the most amazing job. Cody looked so amazing. I am so thankful for people like Cole Houghton, who work their magic on embalming the bodies and preparing them for viewings and funerals. His hair that he had just gotten cut in a new style was done perfectly. They had added a couple of fishing lures to the pocket on his chest and his Angels baseball hat was in his hands. Duane thought of adding in his binoculars around his neck and laying them on his chest.

We set up the foyer with pictures and all of the beautiful plants and flowers that people had sent. We received so many cards and donations. It was so helpful. We did not have insurance because Cody had just turned 26 so, we weren't eligible for life insurance because he was no longer a dependent. So, I hope people know just how grateful we are. There were a lot of people in attendance at the viewing and the funeral. When I got up to give my speech, I felt calm and at peace. I had an unbelievable feeling of strength. I had intended at not making eye contact, but instead, I looked up and saw all of the people and it gave me more strength. Kaylee did very well too. Cody's friends Jordan and Kanyon had very nice things to say. It was a beautiful service.

Here is a copy of Cody's Program from the funeral services:

Cover -

In Loving Memory of

Cody Richard Gillette

December 6, 1991 – March 1, 2018

Memorial Service – March 7, 2018

Tate Mortuary – Tooele, Utah

Inside Cover –

In Loving Memory of

Cody Richard Gillette

Son of

Duane and Angie Gillette

Brother of

Kaylee Gillette

Grandson of

Ron and Sherron Gillette, Richard Jackson, and Janice Jackson

Nephew and Cousin of

Aaron (Jacque) Jackson, Aric (Cassie) Jackson, and Debra Gillette

Dallas Jackson, Jordyn Jackson, Chad Buzianis, Tiffany Nickolas, and Zachary Buzianis

My Dearest Son

You are my greatest wish come true,

Oh, how I love you!

With your eyes so blue,

And your smile so true.

I wish you peace in heaven from here on through.

Love Always ~AG

Insert –

Gone Fishing

I've finished life's chores assigned to me,
So put me on a boat headed out to sea.
Please send along my fishing pole
For I've been invited to the fishin' hole.
Where everyday is a day to fish.
To fill your heart with every wish.
Don't worry, or feel sad for me,
I'm fishin' with the master of the sea.
We will miss each other for awhile,
But you will come and bring your smile.
That won't be long you will see,
Till we're together you and me,
Be happy as I go out to sea.
If others wonder why I'm missin'
Just tell 'em I've gone fishin'.

**WHEN TOMORROW STARTS
WITHOUT ME**

When tomorrow starts without me,
And I'm not there to see;
if the sun should rise and find your eyes
All filled with tears for me;
I know how much you love me,
As much as I Love you.
And each time that you think of me,
I know you'll miss me too.
So when tomorrow starts without me,
Don't think we're far apart.
For every time you think of me,
I'm right here, in your heart.

-David Romano

Back inside cover – **Memorial Service**

Wednesday, March 7, 2018

4:00 PM

Tate Mortuary

Order of Service

Family Prayer Stephen Manzione

Pallbearers

Aaron Jackson, Aric Jackson, Scott Prescott, Kanyon Anderson, Jordan Lund, Josh Bennett, Andrew Pederson and Kevin Anderson

Honorary Pallbearers

Zachary Buzianis

Dallas Jackson

Ryan Allie

Conducting Pastor Rick Ehrheart

Opening Prayer Pastor Rick Ehrheart

Eulogy Kaylee Gillette (sister)

Musical Number

Speaker Gary Brunson (friend)

Speakers Jordan Lund & Kanyon Anderson (friends)

Musical Number

Speaker-Angie Gillette (mother)

Video Tribute

Closing Song-Amazing Grace Everyone

Closing Prayer Pastor Rick Ehrheart

Many special thanks to the outpouring of love and support that we have received! Words cannot express our gratitude and love. Thank you! Friends and family are welcome for food provided by Lane Marshall, Gina Ruiz, and the wonderful ladies of Mountain of Faith Lutheran Church at LaRue and Shirley's 30 W 100 S (right across the street from the mortuary) from 5:30 to 7PM.

Back cover and obituary:

Cody Richard Gillette

1991-2018

Our loving son and brother Cody Gillette, age 26, passed away on March 1, 2018 in Stansbury Park. Cody was born in West Valley City, UT, on December 6, 1991, to Leslie Duane Gillette and Angie Jackson Gillette. He graduated from Stansbury High School in 2010.

Cody was an avid hunter and fisherman. He was a natural outdoorsman. He loved the spending time in the outdoors with family and friends. He also loved baseball, soccer, and golf. He was a great friend and kindhearted. He was enthusiastic, a leader and people were drawn to him especially children.

Cody is survived by his parents Duane and Angie Gillette, his sister Kaylee Gillette, his grandmother Sherron Gillette, his grandfather Richard Jackson, his grandmother Janice Jackson, uncles Aaron (Jacque) Jackson, Aric (Cassie) Jackson, aunt Debra Nickolas, and cousins Chad Nickolas, Zachary Buzianas, Tiffany Nickolas, Dallas Jackson, and Jordyn Jackson, He is preceded in death by his grandfather Ronald Gillette and great grandparents.

A Memorial Service will be held on Wednesday, March 7, 2018 at 4PM at Tate Mortuary (110 S Main ST. Tooele). The family will receive friends for a viewing at 3PM on Wednesday, March 7, at Tate Mortuary. After the service Cody will be cremated and his ashes will be spread in the great outdoors.

Many special thanks to the outpouring of love and support that we have received! Words cannot express our gratitude and love. Thank you!

In lieu of flowers the family appreciates donations to an account set up at any Mountain America Credit Union in Cody's name. They will give the donations to a charity in honor of him.

My speech at Cody's funeral...

My Loving Memories of Cody

I want to start by saying...thank you all for your amazing love and support! We will always be so very grateful to all of you! I need to share a quick funny statement and piece of advice that I received from Kaylee before I begin so you will understand as I share my loving memories of Cody.

I remember when Kaylee first started at the U and she had just gotten done with her first class of public speaking...she called me up and said, "Mom, I can't believe it I have to get up in front of everyone a bunch of times in this class and give speeches." I'm like, "Uh, yeah, that might be why it's called public speaking." Well, $40,000.00 and a degree later, she gave me some wise advice that I am going to follow today. She said, "If you want to make it through your speech so that people will be able to understand you, without crying, don't look up." So, that is what I am going to do. Please just know that I am not trying to be rude. It is my great pleasure and honor to share with you some loving memories and to celebrate my son.

I believe that our most precious gift is our children! Children are truly a miracle and every moment spent with them is a treasure. Please take a moment every day to stop......observe, listen, and enjoy children. Duane and I have been extremely blessed to have two amazing children of our own.

I remember wanting and waiting to have a child for what seemed so long after we were married. Then finally, God blessed us with Cody. I remember one of those first nights when he woke up, as I rocked him back to sleep, tickling his cheek and staring into his beautiful blue eyes singing a song I made up, "I love my Cody, yes I do," knowing that he would touch my life in many special ways. He was by my side from that moment on. He was literally attached to my hip cooking and cleaning. He still loved to cook. Those of you that knew him probably remember times after hunting and fishing coming home with him and he would cook you up fresh dove nuggets or something with every spice in the cabinet. Unfortunately, the cleaning part did not stick with him into adulthood. He remained attached to my hip until his last day we had that sixth sense with each other. He always wanted to know where I was and when I was going to be home and I would always get a feeling if something wasn't right.

Cody loved his sister more than anything. There was a while when I wondered if Kaylee was ever going to walk or talk because Cody did everything for her. He taught her so many things…"This is how you do it sissy, Let me help you sissy." He would do anything for his little sissy. Kaylee was so very shy when she was young, but Cody would take her by the hand and talk her through things, lead her, and help her. Later on, he looked up to her and admired her very much. I know he was very proud of her.

Cody had an excitement for life when he was younger that was like no other. He was full of energy. Some of my favorite memories that I would like to share are:

One year he got a play guitar for Christmas and he kept going around saying, "Look, daddy, it's a guitar, a guitar!" Cody loved music. We used to have family concerts and he would sing. He liked all types of music. I remember him singing some Tim McGraw, a little Garth, Tom Petty, his performance of Kid Rock was very entertaining, and when Kaylee and he used to do Backstreet Boys and 'Nsync oh my…awesome! He had his hair dyed a few different colors trying to be the real slim shady. His recent music, I'm not a fan, but I will cherish all of the memories we have around music and I believe music heals the soul for everyone in some way.

I will never forget the times when he would tie his little Big Foot truck or his bike to our boat or wagon. One time he tied the little tikes wagon to his bike with like 5 ropes and drove around the neighborhood to all of the construction sites to get wood to build a tree house (he was always busy building something). He worked on it day after day. When it was done, he came in the house all serious, hammer strapped to his tool belt, and said, "Mom, it's done come and see." So, I go out, climb up and squeeze inside and there are like a million nails sticking out everywhere zigzagging in every direction. I wasn't sure if I should sit down. I was fearful that I may not get out if I went in, but I did, and I survived, and he was very proud. That was at our old house, but I'm pretty sure that it's still there. In fact, I'm pretty sure that treehouse could survive most anything.

Then there is the dreaded sound that mothers hate to hear when their children are playing out in the backyard... the outside water faucet being turned on. So, I go out thinking, what is Cody doing now? Well, he had built his own fishing pond.

Which brings me to a couple of quick fishing stories. I know that many of you have a lot of great fishing stories as well. Fishing was Cody's true passion. We used to talk about how we should have named him "Fisher" instead of Cody.

He was an amazing fisherman, a natural. My bribe for getting him to go to swimming lessons was that if he went, then while Kaylee was at her lesson, he could fish. So, that worked really well. One day, however, we forgot the pole, but have no fear, he goes and finds a stick and some used line in the weeds along the lake with a hook on it and starts fishing. He rigs it up and the next thing I hear is, "Mom, I caught one!"

He had a special gift- he could out fish anyone. I am so glad that I went ice fishing with him just few a months ago. I asked him once what his secret was and he said.........Hmm wait a minute...I'm not sure I should reveal the Cody Gillette secret, but I know he would want me to let all of you know now so you can carry on his fishing legacy so, here it is are you ready? He said, "You have to talk to them and before you release them you have to kiss them and wish them well." Oh, how I love him!

The South Dakota fish story needs to be told. We would go back to my grandparents' house where Cody would spend his time down by the lake fishing. He was the oldest of all of the second cousins. One time, I was up on the top deck and I could hear chanting so, I look down and I see Cody holding the biggest carp that I have ever seen! He's carrying it like a baby and it's almost as big as him. He is followed by all ten of his second cousins chanting "We're going on a fish hunt!"

I also loved to watch Cody play sports. He was an amazing soccer player. I even coached him one season. The years Eddie Clements coached him were the best! I can still hear Eddie yelling, "Gillette" He was awesome, and Cody was like lightening up and down that field. We are a family of golfers there are many great memories there. Baseball holds a very special place in our hearts. Duane you were lucky to have coached him one season. I especially loved the year when Cody was pitching! Even though it was very nerve racking...He would walk the bases loaded every time and then strike the next three batters out. Ugh! The day he pitched a no-hitter was awesome! Our trip to California this past summer to watch his favorite team the Angels play Duane, Kaylee's and my favorite team the Yankees at Angel's stadium was so much fun.

Cody loved the times spent with his dad!! Duane, you are his best friend! He loved you so much! I know that you are in a lot of pain, but I want you to remember and cherish every single memory that you have and keep doing the things that you and Cody used to do together because I know that Cody would want that and I know that he will be there with you every step of the way. Maybe you will catch the biggest lake trout ever at Flaming Gorge this year if you use the Cody Gillette secret. He will be smiling down on you, I promise! You are a great example of a man. You taught him so many things. It was so fun to listen to you both talk about hunting and fishing and watch you both come alive with excitement. I know he is happy and at peace waiting for you to be with him again and continue where you left off.

Cody also loved his time spent with his cousins, uncles, aunt, and grandpas. His two grandpas taught him so much about hunting, fishing, baseball, and golf. His two sweet grandmas were always checking on him. They loved him so much. Aric you and Cody are so much alike, and he knew how much you cared about him. Aaron he always looked forward to doing things with you and the times spent lately have been so very special to him more than you know.

There have been so many posts from his friends about how he has called to check on you or help you or how you have enjoyed your hunting and fishing times spent with him. Thank you for your kind words and condolences. It brings me great comfort to know that Cody has been a good friend to people, that he has been a great teacher, and has helped many people. He loved being around people, friends and little kids. Thank you for all of you that have been a great friend to him!

Cody and I have spent a lot of time together, especially this last year talking. I will forever cherish those times. I know he wasn't always perfect and made some wrong choices, but I am glad that he was able to learn some important things from me about not judging others and trying to understand others even if they have different points of view or ideas and being kind and helpful to others. We spent many late nights talking. I sometimes needed to comfort my adult son as I did when he was a baby that first night home, rocking him, looking into his beautiful blue eyes, tickling his cheek and letting him know that it will be okay. He returned the favor just a couple of weekends ago when I needed some help and advice, he was right there for me!

I know that Cody knew he was loved. I hope that he is in peace. I will miss the words, "Mom, do you want to watch a movie with me?" I will miss the many things that he and I had in common like our love of shoes, style, and matching our outfits that Duane and Kaylee just laughed at us for. We were alike in so many ways and shared a very

130

special bond. I will miss all of these things, but I will always remember his beautiful smile.

Thank you so much for the overwhelming support that we have received! It has been absolutely amazing! We are beyond words! Our hearts are full of love and appreciation for all of you! So, many people have sent their kind words and condolences, brought us food, sent flowers, made donations, asked how they can help, thanks camo crafters, and Ricky for organizing the fishing event in honor of Cody on Sunday. Your kind words and actions will always be in our hearts and never be forgotten!

I want to leave you with some advice from Cody and me …

As life rolls on,

Embrace every moment, and

Scatter all of the kindness you can

Jordan Lund's Speech…

For those of you who don't know me. I'm Jordan Lund, son of Kevin and Jill Anderson and big brother to Kanyon Anderson and London Rupp. I'm saying big brother but really, I'm the biggest baby… so excuse my tears as I'm sure they will be flowing… The reason I bring up my family is because each of us had a role in the last 20 years of Cody's life. It was the spring of 97 and we just had broken ground on our new home. As my Dad worked on the house, London and I would play in the dirt. We had a giant dirt hill and a deep hole. Quite frankly, pretty dangerous for kids to be around… so, naturally Cody showed up. I don't remember there being a moment where we introduced ourselves. We just immediately started "playing" like we had been friends for years. I remember us jumping down in the pit and he picks up a big handful of mud and tells me with the utmost confidence. "This is Indian clay" I remember thinking, I'm definitely being friends with this kid... he knows about Indian clay! Are you kidding me? This is awesome! And that was Cody. He could take the simplest things and make them into a full-blown adventure. Whatever you did with Cody it was that much more exciting. It wasn't long after that Kaylee and London soon found themselves playing in the dirt as well. And so, began the start of a 20 -year-long friendship between four young '90s kids. Like I'm sure most of you here, some of the wild and most memorable memories I have were with Cody. He was always in search for adventure and seeking thrill. Digging up ancient Indian clay soon lead into late night sleep overs, where most of the time, Kaylee and London would join. Where admittedly we rehearsed our dance moves to Backstreet Boys and would secretly enjoy watching the movie London and Kaylee would always want to watch... Spice World. Oh, how we loved Baby Spice! Now remember this is the '90s we didn't have tablets to keep us busy. So, what did we do...? Played day and night. During the day. We built stuff. Jumped stuff. And destroyed stuff. As well, of course, shot stuff. During the night, we'd play night games, from playing capture the flag on the golf course and having Angie teach us kick the can, to doorbell ditching Stephen Manzione we were always finding another adventure. As the years went by, through the friendship between Cody, Kaylee, London and me. A new friend friendship arose between Cody and my little brother Kanyon. Like Cody and I in the '90s, those two were inseparable. Their love for hunting got our families together for countless hunting trips, whereupon I'd shoot my first deer, and watched Cody gut it. Through years of hunting and us kids being such close friends our parents soon found themselves becoming friends with one another as well. Over the many years and even more memories. Two families of different blood. The Andersons and Gillette's became family. Cody even got the chance to play Uncle for a night with my niece Brooklyn a couple of weeks ago. She loved it and immediately loved him. I'm so thankful he got the chance to spend time with her, she is the light of my life. I will admit over the years Cody and I weren't as close as we were in the 90's. Life got busy and we took different paths, but in the last couple of months we started hanging for a little bit here and there. One night, about a month ago, we spent about 3 hours just driving around above Lakepoint. Reminiscing on all of our memories. We both agreed that we were each other's longest friend that we have had. I am so glad I got that chance. So glad that I took the time to catch up and appreciate an old friend. I'll always cherish that ride Cody. Let that be a reminder to take time to catch up with old friends. You never know just how much you will value your time with them. I'd like the end with the last conversation Cody and I had. It was about my cousin Lincoln's funeral. He came like family would... and supported us in our loss. Cody in person expressed how much he loved Lincoln's services. How cool he thought the Choir was. How crazy it was to see how many people Lincoln had touched. He said, "It was amazing how we celebrated his life, and I think Lincoln was looking down, and he was proud." So, I invite us all to celebrate Cody's life. I'm not asking to stop the tears, or to smile at the memories, just let yourself feel the emotions you have, let them rain over you, use it as a way to hold him in our hearts. For every moment we experience now as long as Cody is in our hearts, he will get to experience too. Cody, I just want to say, I too am amazed by how many people's lives you have touched. I know you're looking down on us and I know you're proud. I love you, Cody. And I'll miss the hell out of you.

Kanyon Anderson's Speech...

A couple nights ago as I was going through old pictures of Cody and me, and I really couldn't find one that we weren't in camo and not in the field, it was also tough finding one of the two of us together, and that was because one of us was usually on the other side of the camera. The burning passion for the outdoors we both had brought us closer than brothers. Like many of you, most of my memories with Cody took place either in the marsh, high country, or right in my backyard. We were never inside. I think I've put more miles under my feet with Cody than I have with anyone else... most of those miles straight up hill. He always seemed to make the trail seem like it was just right around the corner, the only problem was he failed to mention how many corners there were. I've been lucky enough to share almost every hunt I've ever been on alongside Cody for the last 18 years. As far back as I can remember Cody has been my hunting buddy. The only person I've spent more time with on the mountain with is my Dad, but even then, Cody usually tagged along. Cody also had a strong passion to help others. Cody helped me shoot my first dove, he helped me pack out my first deer, my first duck, even my first brown shed antler we picked up just last weekend. I'm sure there's plenty of you out there who caught their first fish with Cody or shot their first coyote. Cody cared more about putting a smile on someone else's face than he did his own. Cody was loyal. He was the greatest friend anyone could ask for, always there

134

when you needed him, advice ready to give, and always awake on time for duck hunts. There's a quote I read this week, it's by Robert Ruark and it says, "the best thing about hunting and fishing, is that you don't actually have to do it, to enjoy it. You can go to bed every night thinking about how much fun you had 20 years ago, and it all comes back clear as moonlight." Cody's impact on my life will carry on with me forever. As it will with all of us. So, the next time I'm watching a sunrise on the Great Salt Lake, or riding out a thunderstorm under a pine tree, I'll remember you, and everything you've taught me, it'll all come back, clear as moonlight.

After the service we went over to the reception and the mood really was more of a celebration with some smiles and laughs as people shared their memories of Cody. It really turned out to be a good day that felt right and left me feeling certain that my son was at peace.

The day after the funeral, relatives went home, and we had the weekend to let everything sink in and try to recover from our emotional exhaustion. We all went back to work on Monday and tried to carry on. I think that keeping busy at work helped all three of us. I was too busy to think about things. There were still so many special gifts, cards, and kind words coming from people. My lunch staff gave me the most beautiful clock that I have on the ledge under the wreath from my staff and the picture from the Andersons. One of the parents in my school gave me a mother and son Willow Tree figurine that I also have on the ledge next to a battery operated candle. I've made it my ritual to turn on the candle when I get home, kiss my fingertips, put them up to Cody's cheek on the picture and tell him that I love him. I leave it on all night and then before I leave in the morning, I do the same routine while turning it off. I haven't forgotten a day.

Chapter 10

Surviving the Worst Year of Our Lives

"Courage isn't having the strength to go on – it is going on when you don't have the strength." ~ Napoleon Bonaparte

We carried on the best that we could. Kaylee even brought up going to counseling and she tried it a couple of times. An interesting thing is that some insurances do not cover families going together as a group for counseling. Whatever, don't get me started on the insurance problem in America. It's unbelievable. We are all doing okay and the best that we can. I can honestly say that we are each other's counselors and support.

Going back to work helped because you get too busy to think about "it" every minute. Also, in my case, being around children truly makes me happy. They are so kind and caring. I love my students. I had been the principal at my school for five years and I knew all of my students well so, it was comforting. They made me laugh and they knew why I was gone and they had made me cards that were the sweetest, banners, and would just come up and hug me. I felt like the students, staff, and parents in my school community were my extended family and that was very helpful in my grieving process. I know that Duane and Kaylee have some great coworkers as well that helped them.

One of the things that helped us was hearing stories about Cody in person from people and reading them from posts on social media. He really was a good friend and a kind person like I had dreamed that he would be all those years ago when I was rocking him and singing to him as a small baby in my arms. One of his true friends, Scott came over a few weeks after the funeral, which I was so thankful for. I had been worried about him. He had a good visit with us and he and Kaylee spoke for a long time. I had given Cody's friends some of his jerseys and hats. I took one over to Scott with a note after that night and he sent me a text

that is probably one of the greatest things anyone has ever done for me.

It is something that touched my heart and I will treasure it forever. I am

so very grateful to him for sharing a part of Cody with me that I had no

idea about and to me is one of the most important characteristics a

mother wants in their child shining through in Cody...kindness. I want to

share it with you now.

These are the first texts from Scott on the day of the funeral...

Scott
March 7, 2018

(1/5) I wanted to thank you so much for coming over on Saturday and
seeing how I was doing and how grateful and honored I am that you
asked me to be a pallbearer.

(2/5) It reminded me so much of Cody, in your time of need you took
time to help others and now I see where he got it from and that it
wasn't just Cody that was so awesome, it was the whole family.

(3/5) You truly are amazing people. I didn't know you and Duane
personally, but I always had so much respect for you guys.

(4/5) I just wanted to let you and Duane know that you both raised 2
truly amazing unique people, a one of a kind boy and a one of a kind girl
and I wanted to thank you both for raising the best friend that I ever
had into the person he was.

My response...

(1/1) Scott thank you so much! That means so very much to me! It also means so very much to me that you were his true friend- the one that stuck with him no matter what! You are always welcome in our home. We would love to have you come talk to us. If you ever need anything let us know. I know we are all hurting now, but I truly believe that Cody is at peace. It's going to be hard and it may be hard a week or month or year from now, just know you can still call, text, come over even then. ♥ you are welcome to come early today at the mortuary if you'd like and also you and your family may sit up front with our family

I wrote Scott a letter a month later to check on him.

From Scott on April 13, 2018...

(1/6) Hi, Angela just wanted to see how you're doing and to thank you so much for your letter. I was feeling down until last night and seeing you guys and reading your letter really helped me.

(2/6) I just wanted you and Duane to know that there was a reason I always stuck by my buddy; he was a damn good friend.

(3/6) He had such a big heart and I wanted to tell you about a couple things he did that really touched my heart.

(4/6) One time we were in SL at a 7-11 and we were about to leave and Cody said, " hold on I'll be right back," and went back in the store and when he came out, he had a box of taquitos and a beer.

(5/6) There was a homeless man I didn't even notice sitting on the curb looking like he was having the worst day and Cody went over and gave them to him.

(6/6) When Cody gave it to him, he started crying and gave him a huge hug and I heard him say thank you so much I haven't ate in 3 days and Cody kept hugging him and told him everything would be alright...

(1/2) And another time we were leaving a friend's house and an old lady was trimming her trees and bushes and Cody tapped me on the shoulder and pointed and was like dude let's help her and we went and helped this old lady with her yard work.

(2/2) It's so awesome that I get to say that's My Best Friend.

My response...

Oh, Scott thank you so very much for sharing this with me! This means more to me than anything that anyone could ever tell me! I have always had a very tender spot for homeless people, and it breaks my heart to see them. Knowing that he would do that makes me so proud and so happy and that he would help others like that lady. I am the same way that's how I live my life and I tried to teach him that. Cody and I were so much alike, and I miss him so much. I wish we had more happy times together and that he would have never turned to drugs. I know it hurt him when he thought I was judging him for it, but I was trying to help I really did understand, and I never judge anyone. I try to help everyone. Thanks so much for sharing! Please share anytime. I have stories too.

Life continued on month by month, I'm not sure how we did it, but somehow, we made it through the year. I did a lot of reflecting, writing, reading, and praying. One of the things that I had to come to terms with was my guilt. The other was that I may never know the "why" of this happening to us. Here is a list of my thoughts...

Living With Guilt and Questions

If Only...

- I would have spent more time with him

- I had listened more

- I hadn't worked so much

- I wasn't so worried about my job and the "stigma" of addiction

- I would have bought or given him everything he wanted or needed

- I wouldn't have bought or given him everything he wanted or needed

- I would have given him more help with doctors, rehab, and counseling

- I would have told him and showed him that I loved him more

- I wouldn't have ignored and looked the other way

- I shouldn't have enabled him

- I wasn't too hard on him

- I hadn't doubted him

- I hadn't lost my patience and yelled at times

- I had read to him more

- I hadn't worried about his room being clean so often

- I taught him how to be more responsible and independent

- I would have praised him more

- I would have thanked him more

- I would have said I love you more

- I would have spent more time with him

Healing-Knowing that I did my best

But I did...

- Answer every phone call and text

- Listen

- Stay up late

- Left work when he needed me

- Watched movies and spent time with him

- Invited him to everything

- Bailed him out many times

- Financially supported him

- Helped in every situation

- Sent him to doctors, hospitals, and counselors

- Tried many things to help him

- Took abuse from him

- ALWAYS forgave him

- Understood addiction

- Helped him with school

- Helped him with his jobs

- Cared for him when he was sick, hurting, and detoxing

- Defended him

- Tried to help him be responsible

- Taught him kindness and respect

- Tried to help him succeed and follow his dreams

- Praised him

- Thanked him

- Supported him

- Always stood by him

- LOVED him

Our month by month survival guide...

March 2018

Jerseys, Hats, and Hoodies

We gave away a lot of Cody's jersey's, hats and hoodies to his friends. I think having something special from a person that has passed on helps with the healing process, keeps their memories alive, and keeps them close to your heart. After hearing so many heartwarming stories from his friends, I wanted to do something special and to aide them in their grieving. There were quite a few of his friends that got tattoos in remembrance of him. We also gave some of his friends and family some of his ashes. I got a tattoo myself with his ashes added into the ink on my left side where I used to always carry him. It's a fishhook with his name and heart embedded in the design. Duane and Kaylee joked with me about getting it that I would end up having bad luck like Cody. As I mentioned before, there were a lot of things that Cody brought upon himself through poor decisions, but there were also many times where he seriously has very bad luck. I got it anyway because I wanted to be close to him and carry him with me always wherever I go. There were so many things that we talked about doing and that I wanted to share and do with him that now we couldn't do, but a part of him is always with me. I know that there are some people and religions that frown upon tattoos, but there are also other cultures, religions, and many people that have tattoos that symbolize something important to them or have a special meaning. We need to respect both.

We all dealt with our grief in different ways. I bought several books on the subject and read a lot. It really helped me. I chose to start writing in a journal, which turned into this book. I collected the photos on my phone and made them into an album. I chose to play the album/video every morning as I drink my coffee. I never want to forget his face!

Another way of dealing with this terrible tragedy was that I had to know everything. As hard as it was, I had to know. I think Kaylee was a lot like me in that way. We were told that the autopsy report may take weeks or even months to come in. I called for updates and I received a call that it was ready on March 15, which was sooner than we had thought it would be so, Kaylee and I went in to pick it up in Salt Lake from the Office of the State Medical Examiner. After I signed for it, we took it out to the car to read it and try to make sense of it. It stated manner of death: accident, immediate cause of death: heroin intoxication. In determining heroin intoxication, the following were in the postmortem blood, morphine, codeine, and 6-monoacetylmorphine (these are all found in heroin). The final pathologic diagnoses/toxicology results included: gabapentin- 9.7mcg/mL, acetaminophen- 7.9 mcg/mL, diazepam- 270 ng/mL, nordiazepam- 190 ng/ml, alprazolam- 75ng/ml, codeine- 21ng/ml, morphine- 270ng/mL, and 6-monoacetylmorphine-9.2 ng/ml. It goes on to explain a detailed analysis of each specimen and to break out the findings by referencing and explaining symptoms of overdose for each substance in "subjects" (people) that were studied or researched. Kaylee had wondered about if there was fentanyl involved, but there wasn't any in his system. I've read it over and over trying to form the best understanding that I can of it. Is it true? Again, I need to come to allow myself to accept the conclusion, that it was an accidental overdose and I will never know why on that day, at that time, Cody decided to put all of those things in his body at once when he had been doing so well, and was looking forward to a bright future. Why was this the time that took his life, when other times hadn't?

Cody had from time to time wanted to remodel his room and get a new dresser. One of the first things that I was clean his room. I got rid of his t-shirts that I hated that had drug references and we got rid of the "dresser of death." His dresser was black and it had scratches all over it from him chopping up pills to snort. I couldn't look at it another minute.

I bought new bedding and put up positive saying signs. I hung up his Jazz jersey and pictures of him everywhere. In some ways, if someone went in there, they may think it looks like a shrine to Cody. Duane thought it was too soon and that it wasn't "Cody's room" anymore. I turned a lamp on and wanted to keep the door open, but Kaylee can't stand to have the door open. Now, I'm actually glad that we keep the door closed because when you walk in the room it still smells like him! I love it! I never want that smell to go away. In fact, that is where Duane goes a lot to just sit down in Cody's room. It's also interesting that if Avery, our lab that Cody rescued from the shelter goes in there, she goes to the spot where I found him and lays down. So, I think it has helped us all. It's a place of healing and peace.

April 2018

"Let's go Yankees"

In December 2017, I got Kaylee tickets to the Yankees game in Houston for Christmas. She is a baseball fan and a huge Yankees fan and wants to go to all of the baseball parks. In the fall, the Astros and the Yankees had been playing on television and Cody was actually cheering for the Yankees just for her. We have it on video. He is chanting, "Let's go Yankees, Let's go Yankees." He knew about it and I bought three tickets one for Kaylee, one for him, and one for me (Duane didn't have any more vacation time). I thought it was going to be a big surprise, but I found out later that Cody had told her. He could never keep a secret especially for his sister. We were so excited to go.

Neither Kaylee nor I wanted to go at all without Cody. Somehow though we gathered up our strength and went. It was so hard on me. I absolutely love traveling with Kaylee. Even though we don't always like the same things and she is a lot like her dad, she is a go with the flow kind of person so, we can both just go here and there and easily agree on where to eat and what to do. We make an itinerary in advance by investigating the best places to eat and visit, the best coffee shops and we go from dusk to dawn. She doesn't mind shopping even though she doesn't buy much (which is good she's responsible with her money), but we have fun. She is the best! I hope to go on many more trips to many more ballparks with her. I'm not going to lie however; it was so hard not to break down and cry at everything we did. I was missing Cody so much. I was in a constant conflict of missing my dead child and trying not to show it while making sure to be present for my living child and enjoy the moment with her. We went to the game, I could tell she missed him too, we talked about it and she played the video of him chanting, "Let's go Yankees."

We also went to the Kemah Boardwalk. Interestingly enough, I was randomly reading my horoscope that morning and it said, I kid you not that I should go to a psychic. When we parked our car and started walking toward the boardwalk there was a big sign lit up that said "psychic" so, we went. This is the first time that Kaylee or I had ever done anything like this so, we were skeptical, but she did tell us some interesting things. I hate roller coasters, but I had to go with Kaylee on the 'Boardwalk Beast" one of the fastest roller coasters in the world because she said that is what she and Cody had planned. I was terrified, but I did it. It was fast!!! Whenever I would go on trips, I would buy Cody a hat as a souvenir. I kept up the tradition and bought him a Houston Rockets hat and it's sitting on his bed.

When we got home my dad had started to have some major incidents with his dementia like driving off to the airport, losing his car, wandering his neighborhood with no shoes on, calling at all hours of the night because he had lost things, and not eating. So, I moved him in with me.

May 2018

Happy Mother's Day?

I was dreading Mother's Day for a couple of reasons. One was that we had another trip planned to go to Las Vegas to see U2 and Cody was supposed to go with us. Another trip that he was looking forward to that he wouldn't be on. Another hole in my heart. Actually, at this point, I'm not sure that my heart was even beating anymore. When you lose a child, you just walk around numb going through the motions. You don't really feel anything anymore except sadness. The other reason was what kind of mother was I that I even deserved to celebrate Mother's Day? After all, I had let my child die.

Well, we went anyway. The concert wasn't very good. We are fans of the U2 Joshua Tree songs and they didn't even play one of those songs. So, besides the concert being long and not good and missing Cody, we tried to make the best of it. We stayed in New York New York, which was fun, we hadn't stayed there before. Our 30th anniversary was coming up in July, which is a pearl anniversary so, Duane bought me some pearl jewelry. He also got me a really special Mother's Day gift. They had a place where you can have a picture laser-engraved into glass. So, I have a picture of Cody and Kaylee together on a crystal heart that says, "Our Greatest Gifts," and it's on a light-up base. I love it!

It wasn't until the end of May that we contacted the Tooele County Sheriff's Office to see if they had any further information on the case. Duane and Kaylee had been asking me often if I had heard anything, but I hadn't and I figured that the sheriff's department and investigators were doing all that they could in the investigation. However, with their insistence, I made some calls, signed the gramma paper, and was able to get Cody's phone back along with the police report. As I read through the report, it stated everything that I already knew. I was able to read the summary of the transcript of the 911 call. The last page stated... manner of death: accident, immediate cause of death; heroin intoxication, case closed. Just like that.

It wasn't case closed just yet however, because also, in May we were in contact with the FBI and DEA. I will touch on this here, but elaborate on it more in Chapter 14, Duane and Kaylee were still very angry at the people that sold Cody the drugs and at the police for not doing anything in her mind since she hadn't heard anything, and for closing the case without making any arrests. It was clear to us who had been a part of it. I, on the other hand, had no anger and I understood that everything that they had was probably circumstantial. However, there was something telling me to follow this through in every and any way that we could and to do the best that I could for my son. We met with them and in our home and an investigation pursued, which is all that I am going to say at this time.

June 2018

On the Lake Again

We always go to Flaming Gorge on Memorial Day and this year

was no different. It was very odd to be on the boat fishing without Cody.

It just isn't the same without him. I miss his excitement when he yells,

"fish on," and how he is smiling and truly in his happy place. It was very

sad, but the three of us had a very special moment of bonding and a

special experience that day as we took the time to remember Cody.

My dad was getting worse however, and was doing very strange

things. His dementia had him not sleeping, not able to do the basic

things to care for himself, and doing very psychotic things behaviorally.

To top it off my mom had fallen and broke her neck the day before we

left, I wasn't going to go, but they put her in the hospital and my

brother stayed with her for those two days. Duane's mom had suddenly

gotten sick, too. Looking back however, I think that my dad's dementia

had been going on and Cody dying caused him to have some kind of

psychotic break. Duane's mom had lost his dad the previous July and

was lonely, but she would come to our house and seem fine on minute and sick the next. However, it was the same thing with her, I believe that she just could not handle the loss of her grandson. She was also officially diagnosed with dementia and hospice was called in.

July 2018

"Ain't No Mountain High Enough"

Sherron's dementia moved so quickly, she quit walking and eating, became incontinent, and she would tell us that she could see Cody and Grandpa climbing the mountain together hand in hand and that they were reaching out their hands for hers. I truly believe that when people are close to dying that they can see their loved ones trying to help them pass. She loved Cody and Ron so much, but she loved Duane and Kaylee very much too. I told Duane to tell her that it was alright to go. I know that she died of a broken heart. I was on my way back from Florida at a principal's conference when it happened. I'm so sorry that I wasn't there for Duane. I had everything ready, by now I was becoming a professional funeral planner. We had her funeral on July 16th and I think it is just how she would have liked it.

We were also able to go fishing to Jordanelle for a day. It was so nice and peaceful to be out on the boat and the water. I spent the time in the sun at the front of the boat reading and writing while Duane helped my dad fish. I was planning a community event. I wanted to organize some type of fishing event for charity. I want to set up a foundation and give scholarships to struggling kids and to those struggling with addiction. I was planning a "Wild About Community" event. It is next on my list after writing this book. It was on that day however, that I found out that one of my friend's son had died by suicide. I was in shock! I just couldn't believe it. I knew him and I would have never suspected it. More than that though my heart was breaking for her because I knew exactly how she felt. So, I started thinking about how I could help her and then I got to thinking about how many other mothers that I knew who had lost a child. I could think of at least 10 in our community and all of them are boys. Sadly, that number has increased since that day.

I decided that I was going to start my own support group. I would call it HOPE. It would stand for **H**elping **O**ther **P**arents **E**ndure. I would have monthly meetings at my house and we could talk and help each other with no pressure or judgment. We would be able to truly understand each other.

I spent a lot of time caring for my dad that month, he couldn't really be left alone. We were going to this doctor and that doctor to try to figure things out. I was also taking classes to get my STEM endorsement. The good thing was that I could now do an online class. The bad thing was that it was math and I am not good at math! I also spent a lot of time with my mom. We had her at the Rocky Mountain Rehabilitation Center. I went to see her every day.

July 1st was our 30 year anniversary. Wow! I had been married for more than half of my life. We were able to go out to a nice dinner at Ruth's Chris Steak House. We had a nice time for a few hours there weren't any tragedies to think about.

Somehow, we juggled everything and we were still able to go on our cruise to Alaska. This was another trip that we had booked a while ago for our anniversary and that I was now feeling guilty about because Cody would have absolutely loved going to Alaska. We were taking Kaylee and we had a lot of fun excursions planned in the ten days that we would be gone. It was an amazing trip. Alaska is absolutely beautiful with the clean fresh air, breathtaking glaciers, and green untouched wilderness. We rode in a helicopter, went dogsledding, panned for gold, and went to a trapper's village that Cody would have loved. The whole time Duane kept saying that he really doubted that we would see Mt. Denali because it was so high that the top third is usually covered by clouds 75% of the year. I had a feeling well actually; I could hear Cody's voice inside my head telling me not to worry that we would see it. I didn't say anything. I thought Duane and Kaylee would make fun of me or think I was CRAZY. I talked to Cody all of the time and I could hear his voice in my head all of the time, but at that time I didn't realize that these were signs and the connection that I had with him.

When we were in Ketchikan there was a bird that kept following us. It was really cool. I will talk about in a later chapter that birds are a sign meant for Kaylee. I could feel Cody's presence/spirit with us on our trip. It was a happier trip than the ones before it.

When were on the train on the way to the Denali lodge the clouds cleared for a bit and we were able to see Mtn. Denali. On the day of the riverboat tour Duane and Kaylee kept saying that we weren't going to see it and I just smiled and let them know that I was sure that we would because Cody would want us to. When we were on the river boat tour on our way back from the trapper's village, I had a feeling and

I looked over to the side where the mountain was and I said, "Hey, is that the mountain?" and there it was. The guide stopped the boat and everyone looked on with awe and excitement. I just smiled with tears in my eyes. I shared my story with a lady next to me and she hugged me. It was a sad, but happy time. I was sure of this moving forward from that day on, Cody is with me and he wants me to enjoy life so, he can enjoy it right along with me. That gave me a new outlook on life. Lookout August! I also turned 50 on July 25th while we were on our cruise. Time to live life to the fullest.

August 2018

"Live Like You're Dying"

We came back and were rejuvenated and ready to celebrate Cody. We had Utah Wildboys t-shirts made with a saying on them, " Living the dream" and "Forever in our hearts and always having our back- in memory of the original Utah Wildboy Cody Gillette.' We didn't sell them for profit, just at cost to whoever wanted them (around a couple hundred). It's really cool when people post pictures on the

Facebook page wearing the shirts or hoodies. I know Cody is smiling.

Kaylee's birthday was July 31st and I wanted to do something special for her so I planned a surprise birthday brunch for her and invited all of her friends. It was really fun. She has amazing friends. They have really been a great support system for her.

We also attended the Fallen Brothers charity golf tournament. Kaylee and Duane golfed with Cody's friend Josh and his dad. The tournament is put on by a man who lost his son to suicide. They donate the entry fees to his foundation The Fallen Brothers. There is also a silent auction and t-shirts with loved ones names on the back in the shape of angel wings. The front says −"excuse me while I change the world," and there is a no bullying symbol on the sleeve because he goes around to schools to speak. I was able to talk to him about getting help and advice on setting my foundation.

On August 11th, I went skydiving with two colleagues. I was scared, but not super scared because I have always had the attitude that when it's your time to die, it's your time to die. I am not afraid of death. It's a natural part of life and I believe in God and heaven so; I know that there is a better place waiting for me. It felt right and it was on my bucket list, I'm not sure why I guess it's because that's what people put on their bucket lists and what they do when they turn 50. I'm not quite sure if Cody would have gone with me or not. Anyway, the main reason that I stayed calm and had no thoughts of backing out was that at this point in my life (I'm being totally honest here) I didn't really care if I died. I had lost my son and that was the worst thing that could ever happen to me besides losing my daughter so if I didn't survive then I would get to see my son again sooner. When we arrived, it was windy and we had to wait. Our jump was postponed for an hour. It was then that I realized that the timing of this was probably not good and that I was being selfish. Duane had come with me. I had thought for support, but in watching him I could tell that he was very nervous. What was I doing? He had lost his father, his son, and his mother all in a year and here was his wife as he had been telling everyone about to jump out of a perfectly good airplane.

The time came. We boarded our little plane and went up just past 10,000 feet. The first pair went then it was my turn. I didn't have time to chicken out. It happened so fast. I think I was pretty much pushed out. At first, I hated it. We had paid for a video so, the girl filming was trying to get me to make heart shapes with my hands and thumps up signals, but I seriously could not breathe. It took my breath away. I was gasping for air. I later asked the ladies that went with me if the same thing happened to them and they didn't experience it. I thought it was strange, but didn't think anything of it until later when I was hiking that high and had a similar experience. It was then that I realize that I get altitude sickness. We did not stay at that elevation very long. We were doing flips and falling then our parachutes opened. When we were down lower and slowly floating to the ground, it was amazing! The feeling is so cool. I am really happy that I did it. My landing wasn't the prettiest due to my bad knees, I sort of landed on my butt. Duane was relieved. It was an amazing adrenaline rush! I can see how some people like to do it again and again.

The next week I was back to work at our opening leadership meetings. They were a little hard for me. With the growing number of children and adults in our country suffering from anxiety and depression, mental health is a topic at the forefront of education. We have been seeing an increase in children's behavior at younger and younger ages. Our topics of the training were about being student-focused and how to help children with mental health issues and who come from trauma. We talked about the importance of building relationships, restorative justice, and getting to know the why behind a student's circumstance rather than just suspending them and forgetting about it. On the one hand, I was very excited because this has always been my philosophy and approach, on the other hand, it was very upsetting to me because I was sitting in the same room with my peers, who had not done any of these best practices when it came to my son and some of them had been recognized and been given awards for their work. It was hard. I remained professional and I have never mentioned the incident except only to a few people without any names being used until now and I will keep the names anonymous. I hold no grudges and I am sure that I have made mistakes in my career. Please know that I do respect my colleagues and I love working for my district. There is not a perfect school or district anywhere and there were certainly many other factors that were involved in my son's problems as I have mentioned.

One of our training days was a teambuilding day at the bowling alley. It was fun, but as I was leaving the bowling alley, I was still upset. I don't know if it was because things were finally sinking in or what. They say sometimes grief will hit you really strongly well, it did that day. As I got in my car, I cried. Then I pulled myself together and went to Walmart even though I didn't want to, but I needed something for the next day. I almost just went home instead. In Walmart, I met someone

that I hadn't seen for a long time. I was in an aisle and there was

another lady. I glanced over at her and she looked familiar, but I didn't

say anything. Then she called out my name and came to hug me and tell

me that she was sorry about Cody. I had taught her son in sixth grade

and he had been friends with Cody. I asked how he was and I was sad to

hear that he had gone through his own struggles, but was doing better.

We talked for about 45 minutes. She brought up that her sister was a

medium, which was odd because I had been thinking about going to a

medium after someone, I knew had told me about their experience and

how it had brought her peace. I told her that and she said it was

interesting that I had been thinking about it and that we happened to

meet there in that Walmart today because she hadn't been there for

years and wasn't going to stop and neither was I. She gave me her

sister's number. I decided to call her to set up an appointment. I will

share that experience in a later chapter.

September 2018

Friends Reunited and Rocky Mountain Climbing

Earlier that year I had found my best friend from when I was five years old and living in South Dakota on Facebook and we had been messaging back and forth. She lives in New Jersey now. Well, New York has always been a dream of mine and of course, Kaylee wanted to go to Yankee Stadium. I have a wonderful husband, who when I said that I wanted to go to New York was totally on board with it. The very unfortunate part of Duane losing both of his parents was that there was insurance money that allowed us to pay off things and to travel. We would of rather of had them still in our lives, but we have been able to experience some new and awesome things.

We had an amazing time in New York. Spending time with Pam was like we had never been apart. We were able to talk and laugh with each other. She was an outstanding hostess. Kaylee loved her. It was a dream come true. Cody and I had talked about going to New York. He would have loved it.

When we got back a couple of teachers on our school wellness committee had organized a hike up Deseret Peak. It is known to be a pretty rough hike. The elevation is 11,035 feet. Cody had done it and we have pictures of him doing it so, I wanted to do it. Duane came along.

I'm not sure if it was because he wanted to do it, or if it was because he was afraid that I would not make it. I have two bad knees (one that I have had surgery on), a bad hip and two feet that I've had surgery on. I'm a mess basically, not to mention overweight and out of shape. As we pulled up in the truck early in the morning, Duane still nervous, and turns to me to let me know that I could still back out and the song that was played at Cody's funeral came on the radio, "See You Again," well to me that was a sign that I needed to do it for my son. He gave me strength yet again. Now, I was determined more than ever. I am the type of person that when I say that I am going to do something, I do it. If I put something on a list, I complete it. If I set a goal, I do not give up until I reach it. It's my personality. I'm a type-A, worrying/blue, perfectionist, OCD, overachiever. The thing that will always haunt me forever, is that I failed as a mother. I certainly didn't overachieve there. It took all day, but we made it to the top. As we went to turn the final switchback however, the wind was blowing and we were at around over 10,000 ft. The same thing that had happened to me when I was skydiving happened again, I couldn't catch my breath. It was scary. I sat down for a few minutes and tried again because it was just a bit further, but I couldn't breathe. So, we headed back down. Duane said that he was still proud of me. He didn't think I would make it that far. I've always said that the most painful thing that I have ever experienced is a kidney stone, followed by natural childbirth, then climbing Deseret Peak comes in third for me.

October 2018

HOPE

October was a hard month. It was a month of hunting in Utah therefore, it should have been a happy time for Duane, but without his best hunting buddy, he was feeling depressed. However, just like old times, I decided to go with him to deer hunt this year. We packed up the trailer and headed west to the Stansbury Mountains to the hunting spot where Cody had gone last year. It was located on the backside of the same mountain range as Deseret Peak, which we had just climbed. Again, just as we pulled into our camping spot, we got a sign from Cody as "See You Again," stared to play on the radio. We both looked at each other and smiled. We set up camp and Duane took me for a four wheeler ride to where Cody had harvested his buck the year before. I have enjoyed going to all of the places that my son has been to. It makes me realize even more what an amazing person he was. I wish that I would have gone with him more. I'm not sure that I could have kept up with "The Legend," but I'm sure that he would have helped me every step of the way and made sure that I was safe and taken care of. Duane did not get a deer.

I had cried often since the passing of my son. In fact, several times a day was the norm. Most of the times I shed tears of sorrow, some of the times I shed tears of happiness. That's a hard one to explain, but I will give it a try. Parents who have lost a child will understand. You are always sad every moment of every day, but somehow, you kind of go numb and learn to cope and live through life while experiencing it as a shell of a person because you have an outside physical body that can appear to function, laugh, or smile. However, it's like you have an invisible giant hole that nobody sees, in which your heart and insides have been ripped out and you can't feel anything like you used to unless it's a sharp stabbing, gut wrenching pain, or like an empty space full of air. On occasion, you can feel a little twinge of what you remember joy to be an you may shed a happy tear for your lost child because you feel the love you still have for them and you know in your head and heart of hearts that they are at peace and in a better place. You can find comfort in that breathe again and let life roll on. So, even though I had cried and cried hard on some occasions, I hadn't really "broke down" and let it all out and had a raging cry until one night in October. I am thankful for this and I have a great deal of respect for the person who said the kind words to me that for whatever reason triggered this major cry. He doesn't even know this and in more ways than one made a major impact on me that night. I attended a school board meeting, the focus of our district had been on culture and climate of schools, which is extremely important to me and as the board members were having a discussion, he called me out saying what a very positive climate I had built in my school. That my school was very kind and welcoming to all. Relationships with students and all people are of the utmost importance to me so, for him to say this made not only my career goal feel accomplished, but also one of my life goals. I will forever be thankful to him. As I left the meeting that night, it was pouring down rain. I could hardly see to drive and to top it off, thinking about the kind words of the school board member, I just started to sob uncontrollably. I was thinking about yes, I have built relationships and helped so many kids, but I couldn't help and save my own son. I have lived my life trying to be kind and helpful every day to every person that

I meet and God just keeps dumping more and more bad things on me. Why? I almost hydroplaned off the road, I didn't care. I don't care if I die, truth be told. Then I could be with my son again. As I pulled into the garage, I sat there for a few minutes pulling myself together. I used a little self-talk and came to the conclusion...it's all part of God's plan and I'm not going to know why. I need to deal with it the best that I can and continue rolling on the path of kindness and positive vibes only knowing that Cody is at peace and that I will see him again. Sometimes a good long hard cry is just what you need like a good hard laugh to jumpstart you into carrying on .

The next week I went to the medium. It was an amazing experience that helped build my connection with Cody and bring me peace. As I mentioned, I will share that experience later. I can tell you that it gave me strength and hope to carry on.

October is also when I had the first HOPE group meeting. The first meeting was at my house. I had invited around ten people and four people showed up. I didn't have an agenda or a plan and I wasn't really sure how things would go, but we just started talking with no judgments and everyone shared their stories of their precious child that they had lost. They all thanked me for starting the group. It was very helpful to us all. The next month we had three more people come, but in December, which I understand, things kind of slowed down to what we have now, our regular three. I am and always will be forever grateful for these women. They get it! They understand as no one else can. I love and admire them. I have also come to love their sons through their stories of them. I believe that we have a true friendship and bond that will never be broken.

November 2018

Bull Riding

Duane went goose hunting in Wyoming with Kevin and Kanyon, which was another trip that had been planned with Cody, but I was glad that Duane still went and that he was with them. I was determined to ride the mechanical bull. I had tried it once in Washington D.C. and I couldn't jump on it. Then when Duane, Cody and I were in Las Vegas, Cody and I were going to give it a try, but changed our minds so, I had to do it now. Kaylee and I went with some of her friends and mine into the Westerner where they were nice enough to let one of Kaylee's friends boost me up on the bull. Yay! I did it. So, in the words of Tim

McGraw, I was able to "Live Like I Was Dying." I had been posting my

adventures on Facebook all along and a very special person took the

pictures from my posts and made a video of them to that song. It is very

special to me. Never take one moment of life for granted. That is how I

am choosing to live.

Live Like You Were Dying

Tim McGraw

He said
"I was in my early forties
With a lot of life before me
And a moment came that stopped me on a dime
I spent most of the next days
Looking at the x-rays
Talkin' 'bout the options
And talkin' 'bout sweet time"
I asked him
"When it sank in
That this might really be the real end
How's it hit you
When you get that kind of news?
Man, what'd you do?"

He said
**"I went skydiving
I went Rocky Mountain climbing
I went 2.7 seconds on a bull named Fumanchu**
And I loved deeper

And I spoke sweeter
And I gave forgiveness I'd been denying"
And he said
"Someday I hope you get the chance
To live like you were dying"

He said
"I was finally the husband
That most of the time I wasn't
And I became a friend a friend would like to have
And all of a sudden going fishin'
Wasn't such...

And I went three times that year I lost my dad
I finally read the Good Book, and I
Took a good, long, hard look
At what I'd do if I could do it all again
And then

I went skydiving
I went Rocky Mountain climbing
I went 2.7 seconds on a bull named Fumanchu
And I loved deeper
And I spoke sweeter
And I gave forgiveness I'd been denying"
And he said
"Someday I hope you get the chance
To live like you were dying
Like tomorrow was a gift
And you've got eternity
To think about
What you'd do with it
What could you do with it
What did I do with it?
What would I do with it?

Skydiving
I went Rocky mountain climbing
I went 2.7 seconds on a bull named Fumanchu
And I loved deeper
And I spoke sweeter
And I watched an eagle as it was flying"
And he said
"Someday I hope you get the chance
To live like you were dying
To live like you were dying
To live like you were dying"

Thanksgiving is my favorite holiday because I love to be with family and eat good food. It has always been rough though because for some reason Duane makes holidays hard for me. I love to be around family, decorate, and just spend time together. He is more of a loner. Thanksgiving has always been at our house. It is a lot of work, but I don't mind. I make two turkeys. I make one the traditional way in the oven so we can have the stuffing and gravy and the other deep fried because it turns out so juicy. Well, Duane always gives me fits about it. So, this year Cody had told me that he would cook the deep fried turkey. Well, that never happened. In fact, we didn't have anyone over for Thanksgiving. None of us felt like celebrating. Duane and Cody would always go hunting so, I know that Duane was feeling sad. I was sad. I did make a turkey for just us, but it was strange, it was like I forgot how to

cook. I had become very scatter brained. I would be doing one thing and

forget what I was doing in the middle of it. I later read that this is very

normal for parents who have lost a child. I have noticed this happening

off and on over the past year. It's hard to take for me as the person who

has always had it all together and been very organized.

I was able to pull it together enough to do some Christmas

shopping. Duane and I had decided that the money we would have

spent on Cody this year we were going to spend on other in need. I

bought some things for a sweet young mother and her two children that

had been a friend of Cody. I couldn't help seeing things that I wish that I

could have gotten for Cody everywhere. I kind of turned it into a game.

I spent the rest of the weekend just laying around depressed.

December 2018

Happy Birthday to You

Cody's birthday was on December 6th. He would have been 27.

We all went to work that day. With Thanksgiving being so sad. I just felt

numb for Cody's birthday, but thank goodness for Kaylee she insisted that we celebrate so, we went to dinner at Red Lobster, which is where Cody would usually choose and we had a good time.

Kaylee was finally brave enough to get her tattoo in honor of Cody the day before his birthday. It's on her inside forearm with mountains and pine trees and has his initials. She didn't use his ashes though. Ha Ha.

Christmas was low key. I still put up a stocking for Cody and Kaylee had bought me a really nice ornament with his picture on it. My dad was with us and he is one of my favorite people to buy gifts for because he gets excited over everything even socks. I got him a new pool stick to play pool at the senior citizen's center. We had everyone over like we always did for prime rib on Christmas Day and it turned out delicious. I had been reading a book called, <u>Signs From Heaven,</u> since Duane had accidentally ordered me $100 in grief books from Amazon. When I was upset over Thanksgiving weekend, I had put a bunch of books in the cart and he had gone on to order one fishing lure and didn't check before he submitted the order and ended up ordering everything that I had saved in the cart. I am very grateful that it happened because that is one of the best books that I have read. I get

signs from Cody almost daily.

Over Christmas break, we went snowmobiling in the Uintah

Mountains up by Mirror Lake. We stopped at an overlook point to enjoy

the view at one point and a hawk came flying over us. It was really cool.

Duane was really starting to believe me now about my signs and that

Cody was with us. We made snow angels and wrote messages in the

snow to Cody. It was a good day.

January 2019

This Year Has To Be Better Than Last Year

In Kaylee's words *^%# 2018. We said goodbye to 2018 and

welcomed in 2019 by toasting with Cody's favorite drink. After all, 2019

had to be better right?! It snowed and I went outside to build a

snowman and dressed it up in Cody's clothes. We were all hoping for a

new and better year, but it already wasn't looking like that was going to

happen. The health of both of my parents was declining.

January was a pretty uneventful month. Duane and I both had changes in our jobs. His boss that he had really respected and been close with transferred to another state. I had been the principal at my same school for six years and it was becoming a stressful time in education. Many students are having more anxiety, which in turn, causes more anxiety in parents and teachers. A few teachers were struggling so, I needed to become more involved in the behavior management as more students were being sent to the office. As I was meeting with one of them who was struggling, she mentioned that it was because of me not being the same after my son's death. Wow! I had tried really hard to be professional and not let my overwhelming grief affect my job performance and I thought that I was doing quite well. I was quite upset about this comment. If it weren't for the honest words of my area director, my assistant principal, and my lead teacher, I may have left education. I knew that I could trust their feedback and honesty about how I had been handling everything. Also, one morning as I was making the fifteen minute drive to work and pondering life as I do on this commute, I thought again to myself... I've had a great career and it's what I've always wanted to do, but maybe I should move on. Is there something else for me? I had started to feel this uncertainty often in the past few months like this isn't my end path. I can't quite see what is, but it's not education. There's something else, it's not clear to me what, I don't know why. What is God's plan for me now after Cody's death? What am I supposed to do? I was seriously thinking of leaving the education field in two years for sure. That's when I would have my full thirty years in and could retire, or maybe calling that day to find out about the cost of buying those years. As I got to work that day, the Superintendent was there to see me. I thought to myself...he never comes to visit, this is odd. It was just a friendly visit. He just wanted to look around the school and talk about how things were going. We ended up in my office first and started talking. We talked for two hours about students and mental health. We talked about Cody and my writing of this book. I was worried about sharing this story and people judging me. He told me to tell my story! He saved my career in education that day. I'm grateful to him for that. I have many more students to love and help. I have parents to meet and help. I have teachers and staff to train to be leaders. I have a new outlook and I was ready to finish out the year strong and make the next year the best ever! I even started considering a change and moving from elementary to secondary to try my best to make a difference there.

February 2019

Fun in Paradise

Duane and I went on a cruise to Mexico. We did a lot of fun things. We swam with dolphins, which was an incredible experience. We went fishing in the ocean. Cody would have loved that. We know that he was there with us that day because we had a single bird flying by the boat the whole time. The guides kept commenting on it. They tried a number of things to get it to go, but it would not leave even when they would feed it. Duane and I just looked at each other and smiled. We renewed our wedding vows. We went ziplining in the jungle. I hated that! It was very scary to me, but Duane absolutely loved it! He kept saying that Cody would have loved it. I agree, he would have. We ate good Mexican food for Cody as we sailed on a sailboat in the ocean whale watching.

March 2020

RIP Cody – UT Wildboy

Well, we made it. I wasn't going to take the day off of work, but Duane and Kaylee wanted to so, I did. We didn't really know what we were going to do. Do you mourn? No. We had already done that and had been doing that every day. Do you celebrate? No, was my thought. I didn't even know what to think. I was not going to have the words, "the first anniversary of my son's death," come out of my mouth. To me that is not a holiday nor a celebration. It shouldn't even be a thing. So, we sat around for a while. Duane and I were pretty lethargic. It was Kaylee that pulled us out of our slump. I had wanted to climb what I had been calling "Cody's mountain," (the one on the cover) and reenact the picture, but we had gotten a lot more snow this winter than last. We decided to drive out there anyway. As we scoped out the area, Duane pointed out the spot to us where the picture of Cody was taken and flying around in circles was a hawk. We watched for a while and as we turned the truck around to leave, two more hawks joined it and they followed us down the canyon...Cody, Ron, and Sherron flying together carefree, having fun, at peace, and letting us know they are always near.

After that, we decided to go shooting guns because that would be a Cody thing to do. So, we went across the Tooele Valley westward to the shooting range outside of Grantsville. One of my friends had sent me a picture in the fall of some graffiti that someone had done on one of the rocks, in which they had spray painted, RIP Cody G. We saw it as we pulled in. There had been more added to other rocks, one said RIP Cody G the original Utah Wildboy. He sure is missed by many. In fact, we had all been receiving messages all day from people thinking of us and missing Cody. There have been so many people throughout the year that have shared their special stories of times with Cody when he was alive and after he passed. It warms my heart each time. Yes, there were those very dark times that only some know about or only know him for, but there were so many really good times that many people know him for. As his mother, he was the child and young man that I had hoped he would be kind and caring. That is the person he really was deep down and I knew that and loved him for who he was. I just wish that he could have realized how many people's lives that he touched and how loved he really was. I wish he would have loved himself enough to have the strength to fight and overcome the devil of addiction.

Later that day, the most amazing thing happened, Kaylee received an interesting message on Facebook messenger from someone that I didn't even know and she knew from high school. Again, some readers may have a hard time believing, but I'm sharing because we have had so many signs and positive experiences and I want people to know the impact that my son has had on others and our lives. Plus, it is part of the story and it has helped my life roll on. This young lady Cody's age had gone to high school with him. It sounded like she didn't even know that it had been one year on this exact day that she sent the message. Here was her message...

"Hey girl, I know it's been a long time, but Cody visited me in my dreams a little while after he passed. It literally was the most amazing, most real, scariest thing to experience. I tried to wake up my boyfriend because I was trippin out at first because he was sitting on my bed talking to me, but he told me not to wake him up and that it was ok. We ate Little Caesar's Pizza and I had an out-of-body experience. It was idk, I don't even know if I have the words. He said to tell my family that I love them and I'm sorry. Now, I don't know how he passed, or what happened, I just know that he is okay and that he loves you so much. I will never forget it and I will cherish it and hold it in my heart forever.

He is an amazing man and has one of the most beautiful souls that I have ever met. Sorry if that was too much, but I had a burning desire to share it with you. That's what Cody would have wanted. He said that he would let me know when to tell you and I felt it was now. Wow, what timing. I love my son!

We decided to go to Olive Garden for dinner. Cody liked that restaurant. It's not my favorite, but it was one of those places that the whole family could agree on if you know what I mean. We went to the one in West Valley. It was hard when we walked in, I felt sick to my stomach, the last time we had been to that restaurant he was with us. I remember him sitting across from me. We had the same thing to eat, of course, a steak pasta dish, because we liked the same things. I really miss him. I remember him that day sitting across from me. That was when he was doing well and we were all having a good conversation. He was smiling and laughing. My heart was happy. Now, I looked across the table and I saw my beautiful daughter, who I'm very grateful for, my dad, who now lives with us due to his dementia, and no Cody. I laid my head on Duane's shoulder my heart hurting. I know he felt the same.

Chapter 11

An Unbreakable Bond

"My mind still talks to you, my heart still looks for you,

but my soul knows that you're at peace."

~ Beauty of Life

From that moment that I first sat singing to Cody in the rocking

chair, looking into his beautiful blue eyes, I knew we had formed a bond

that would never be broken. Our love is strong. It is an unconditional

love. There wasn't anything that he did or said that could make me stop loving him. Through all of the ups and downs, I always stood by him. We have an amazing connection. I could always sense when he needed me and now, he can sense when I need him.

We had so much in common, starting with our personalities. We were both on the sensitive side. We cared a lot about what people think about us and were always hoping for praise and approval. I'm not that way so much anymore. Neither of us like(d) to be alone. We are both social. We had/have empathy and care about the underdog. We both love(d) children. We love(d) fashion, matching, and shoes. We love(d) to watch TV together especially Netflix. They say that when you are pregnant and crave certain foods that you eat a lot, your child will end up eating that same food a lot. I have found that to be true. When I was pregnant with Cody, I craved sweets like Hostess cupcakes and I drank a lot of milk. Cody liked sweets and drank a lot of water and milk. When I was pregnant with Kaylee, I craved hot dogs with mustard (which I had never liked before) and I drank soda (which I hardly ever drank) and Kaylee loves cheese hot dogs with mustard and has always been a pop drinker. There have been so many times when either Duane or Kaylee will say to me, "Okay, Cody," because I will do, or say something that is what he would have said or done and they used to say the same thing

186

to him only saying, "Okay, Angie."

I've already told you about the experience that I had the night before his funeral, where he came to me and gave me strength. I heard his voice and I can still hear his voice inside my head sometimes. It's hard to explain, it is definitely not my own voice telling me things that I think Cody would say. It is him! It is his actual tone and the way he would speak. He gets my attention first a lot of the times like he always did, by saying, "Mom," in his own unique way and then it is followed by whatever it is that he wants to say. I know how this may sound, but I am just telling you honestly how it is. You can believe it or not.

I've also told you about my tattoo with his ashes on my left side. My life continues to have hardship after hardship and as one of my friends recently said you certainly are on the struggle bus. Duane and Kaylee are still convinced that I inherited Cody's bad luck by getting this tattoo with his ashes, but I asked the medium about it and she said that Cody, just laughed about it and said that he wasn't wishing his bad juju on me so, who knows. I do know that I have had enough hardships and I am ready for them to end at any time if you are listening, God.

I oftentimes wonder if I have also taken on the burden of some of his symptoms that he had to deal with. I don't know why I would need to do this, perhaps to better understand what he went through since he would frequently say to me that I just didn't get it even though I would tell him that I did. I have read somewhere that this is a real thing and it's called having identification symptoms. That parents can experience what their child experienced when they died, or maybe in my case when they were living because their connection runs very deep. It's a mystery, but isn't unheard of, rather natural and common as well as certainly spiritual. So, by now, you may be saying, okay, she is definitely crazy! Well, my child died. That's crazy. The world as we knew it is no longer. Cody used to have insomnia. I haven't slept through the night since the day that he died. If I do fall asleep, I often wake up at 1:30, which is the time I woke up that terrible night in March and found him dead.

I've also read somewhere that when our loved ones go to Heaven that they are able to see everything past and present from other's viewpoints so, I think he is now able to see the things that he said and did, both good and bad and know how they impacted us, made us feel, and wants us to know that he is sorry by sending us signs.

I didn't really know what these signs were until after I went to see a medium on October 23, 2018. After speaking with her, and buying a couple of books about signs from a loved one in Heaven, I started to notice and feel Cody's presence. He is always with me. Our bond is truly unbreakable. I will share the many signs that he has given us in the next chapter, but for now, I want to share what the medium had to say. You may or may not want to read on with the rest of this chapter. I share this because it is a part of my experience, my healing, and it is a part of my bond with my son. I know that some may judge me for it, some may think I'm "crazy", but it is what it is. I'm not sure what is the right thing to do and what is wrong when you lose a child. I do know that I now believe that my son is in a good place, he is with me all of the time, I believe God is good with it, and it is what keeps me strong.

So, if you will recall, in a previous chapter I mentioned running into a lady in Walmart, who mentioned that her sister was a medium. I felt that the coincidence of that meeting was telling me that I should call her and set up an appointment. So, I did. However, after I did, one night shortly after, I woke up at my usual 1:30 and went out into the family room to google mediums. As I was reading, something struck me that there may be beliefs that this was against my religion. So, for the next few days, I was feeling uneasy about going. I asked some other family members' and friends' opinions on what they thought about it and everyone thought it was okay, but I still felt uneasy so, I called my Pastor. He is a great man. He is the one I turned to after Cody died. I called him and he met me and we talked for a couple of hours and then after the funeral, we met again and talked. I trusted him. So, when I asked him about the medium, he told me pretty much what I had read that it was something that wasn't encouraged because as the Bible said there could be evil spirits that are spoken to or called forth. So, I had decided not to go.

Then I went to work and just before my appointment was supposed to be, I spoke with a good friend and asked her about it. At the spur of the moment, she said she would go with me so, off we went. It was October 23, 2018. I went with an open mind, but somewhat skeptical because after all, she did know me and Cody as well as our situation. There was also, my religious background. Since I am honest, I was upfront with her on all of that from the beginning, and she spoke to all of it and made me feel at ease. We sat of the couch and the medium took a few minutes to get to know me and ask a few questions like when my birthday was and things like that. She said that she could see positive energy and colors around me of orange, violet, and teal with green sparks for healing. She said that I was an empath and that I take on other's emotions. I am very intuitive toward other people's feelings and that I am understanding. That is very true.

She started out by saying that she was seeing some darkness. I listened intently, She said it was not from me, but it was Cody and he was feeling guilty. Then she asked me if Cody had ever stolen a car? I told her no, but my friend whispered to me about the Porsche. I explained that he had taken Duane's car without asking first because he was out of gas and totaled it. She said that he felt tremendous guilt for that and selling/pawning a gun of his. I told her to tell him that we didn't care about a dumb car.

She told me that Cody was always with me. He puts me on a pedestal. He is my guardian angel and just as I was always his angel. He will never leave my side just like I never left his -no matter what. I was the one that never gave up on him. I did all that I could and put my foot down. He said to tell me that it was an accident and that he had been trying a long time to do well and was. It's not my fault. It was his choice. He is happy and at peace now. He is with his Grandpa Ron. She asked if another death had occurred recently and I told her yes, his grandma Sherron. She said that he had helped through and that she was content now.

Then she asked if I had any feelings or signs of him around. An intuition? I told her about the night before the funeral, but I hadn't noticed any signs? She asked about feathers and numbers on the clock. No, I hadn't noticed those. Feathers, really, I never see feathers? Songs? Yes, we had all noticed that. I had noticed quite frequently that the song we played at Cody's funeral "See You Again," would play at just the right moments when I was feeling sad, thinking of him, needing some encouragement, or when something was about to happen. I let the song play and enjoyed it. Duane and Kaylee couldn't yet handle it. She said that they needed to because that was Cody's way of communicating with them. That he rides in Duane's truck beside him.

She made mention of some things like my spirit guide and how I was going to speak in front of a lot of people. Also, how I would talk to a group of others about Cody (I didn't even realize that night was my first HOPE group meeting). There is no way she could have known that or about the car and guns.

That night at my HOPE group meeting, I opened a brand new package of napkins, passed them out with treats, and on my napkin was a tiny purple feather right when I was about to share the story of my son. My first of many feathers.

Oh, the signs! I began to be flooded with signs from my dear son! I ordered a book from Amazon, "Signs From Heaven," and maybe it was me becoming more aware, but Cody was there. He is with me all of the time. At first, I didn't keep track, then I started writing them down in a journal or on my phone. Then I started to notice what was going on when I would get a sign. It's truly amazing! He is my guardian angel! He is here for me when I need him. He gives me strength, hope, and peace.

After a while, Duane and Kaylee became believers, too. I had asked them to just open their eyes and have a little bit of an open mind. In fact, Cody is all over the place communicating with everyone, which makes me happy because that's who he was, an empath himself. He was always wanting to help others and let them know that it would be okay. In March, Kaylee was interested in going to the medium herself so, we went together. It was March 19, 2019, this time I let her speak to Kaylee first. She started out by saying that Cody wanted her to know that he loves her so very much, is very proud of her, she is beautiful, and that he had wanted to be the best brother to her that he could be, but he was so very sorry that he failed. He wanted her to know that he loved her tattoo (Kaylee got a tattoo of mountains and Cody's initials) and that it was cool that she went shooting. This was something the medium couldn't have known? We asked some questions this time like what we should name our new puppy and if Cody had taken the few items that were missing around the house. A few good things came out of this session, one was that we were right that it was meant to be me that found Cody that night of his death and not Kaylee. That we couldn't have saved him. That Kaylee will go on to have a good life and her brother will be with her. His signs to her are in nature. She sees birds a lot and knows that because of the timing they are from him. We recorded the session this time and played it for Duane and we had a breakthrough in the events of that night and everyone's thoughts and feelings. Both times there has been mention of a grandchild from Kaylee...hmm, I'm still waiting for that!

Chapter 12

Signs From Heaven

"When angels are near, feathers appear."

~Unknown

I am a firm believer that there are angels among us. I have

always believed this, but now I know it! I don't think that my eyes and

mind would have been open to this had it not been for my visit to the

medium and my reading of books about other's experiences. I have

always been a very spiritual person and I do believe in what I have read in the Bible about visits from angels and the teachings/sermons given by my pastors over the years. I did experience something when I was younger, a visit from my grandfather and I do believe myself to be in tune with others. I didn't realize that I may be an empath until a short while ago, but it makes sense to me now. However, I have never been so aware and in tune with my surroundings, cued into my senses and certain that my son is near.

I've shared with you some of my experiences and signs from the night before Cody's funeral to some of the things that happened after the visit to the medium. Here are some more. I could go on and on. It's an almost daily occurrence that Cody shows me in some way that he is with me, supports me, or gives me the strength to carry on. It's not just me, he is everywhere. There have been many people that have reached out to us with stories about how he has contacted them in some way like through a dream or another sign. Each time he had a message to give them and many times a message for them to give us from him. It truly is amazing. It may sound crazy and many who read this may not believe it, but I know it to be true. I know that not everyone who has a loved one pass away is fortunate enough to have this type of connection or receive signs from a loved one, but to them, I say this...one day you will see them again and that is the hope that you

need to hang on to.

Here are some of the signs from when I decided to keep track in my

phone notes (these don't include when I take a screenshot of the many

times, I go to look at the time and it is a triple digit number)...

- 4/2/19-a tiny purple feather on my desk at work
- Easter 2019- a tiny white feather
- 5/1/19-5:55
- 5/ 2/19- kitchen lights flicker and 1:11
- 5/3/19- 5:55
- 5/24/19- "See You Again" came on the radio
- Sunday before Memorial Day 2019 ashes and 12:12
- 5/28/19-3:33 woke up
- 5/29/19-3:33 woke up
- 6/1/19-woke up at 1:30 -3:33 -found a blue feather
- 6/5/19 -4:44
- 6/13/19-2:22
- 6/18/19-2:22- 3:33- 4:44
- 6/19/19-5:55
- 6/28/19- woke up at 1:11 lights flicker
- 6/28/19-2:22- 4:44- saw feather clouds
- 7/1/19- woke up at 11:11and hummingbirds all month long
  3 of them always together
- 7-15/19- 2:22- talking to Ann about heroin and addiction
  Then 3:33 on my way to assisted living
  Also heard "Live Like You Are Dying" and "See You
  Again" songs on the radio at
  5:55 after signing dads papers
- 7/16/19- 3:33

- 7/21/19- a feather in my path at a restaurant in AZ
- 7/23/19 - woke up at 5:55 - dad called me in AZ
- 7/25/19- 5:55 -support- hard day with dad feeling guilty
- 7/25/19- 5:55- moved dads stuff into memory care
- 7/28/19-11:11 woke up only my power to my alarm clock went off twice
- 7/30/19- 2:22 and 3:33
- 8/3/-4:44
- 8/4/19- 5:55 -1:11
- 8//19-2:22
- 8/8/19-5:55
- 8/18/19- a feather in a portable at work- 4:44
- A lot in August almost every day
- 9/3/19-4:44 and 5:55
- 9/6/19- two feathers one with a difficult student
- 9/7/19-2:22 right when I was typing a message to help teachers
- 9/17-3:33
- 9/20/19- 4:44 and 5:55
- 9/23/19-11:11-3:33-5:55
- 9/25/19- 11:11- 2:22
- 9/26/19- 3:33- "See You Again"
- 9/27/19- 1:11- 2:22 - "See You Again"
- 9/29/19-3:33
- 9/30/19-5:55
- 10/1/19-5:55
- 10/4/19- 2:22-3:33
- 10/6/19-5:55
- 10/8/19-11:11
- 10/12/19- 4:44-5:55- 11:11
- 10/13/19- 11:11
- 10/11/19-pennies(first time for that) feather
- 10/14/19-5:55
- 10/15/19-1:11
- 10/17/19-11:11
- 10/28/19-4:44- a fishhook cloud

- November 2019- 3:33 a lot and 4:44 -2:22
  Feather in garage
  Feather in Jeff's car
  Feather at school
  **11/30/19- 2 days after Thanksgiving - I was having a
  very rough time- my cardinal snow globe turned itself on
  4:44- 2:22-3:33-4:44
- 12/2/19-2:22-5:55
- Daily numbers
- 12/6/19- we went to stay at a lodge and snowmobile for
  Cody's birthday- I kept waiting for a sign- nothing
- 12/7/19- opened the curtains and a blue jay appeared on the
  porch of our cabin

I wish that I would have taken the time and written down what
was going on in the moment that I received each sign, but I can honestly
tell you that for each of these times the sign from Cody was a message
for me that was very much needed. They came as a message to hang in
there and keep going at a struggling moment or as a reassurance that I
was doing the right thing.

Duane is still very skeptical of the triple digits on the clock. He
says that it happens twice a day every day. He is correct, but I always
ask him if it happens to him often, or randomly when he picks up his
phone to check the time, and at times when it is clearly needed and his
response is always a no. He never sees the same triple digits. I call them

angel numbers. When I look at the numbers that are a sign from Cody, read the meaning, and consider the circumstances of the moment, it makes sense to me. Everyone is free to believe as they wish, all that I can say is I can't explain it, but it's the same as mother's intuition, he is near me all of the time. I know it. Our bond was and remains that strong.

In case you are wondering what some of the numbers or signs mean here is a short synopsis for you...

I started to research angel numbers and this is what I found out: numbers come from early philosophers and are the language of the Universe. They can be found in the core make-up of everything and they vibrate on a level that constructs worlds. Each number has its own frequency and when you observe repeating numbers in a sequence you are receiving Divine guidance. These patterns and sequences are referred to as Angel numbers. You will see them when angels are trying to communicate with you or get your attention. According to sagegoddess.com, the sequences mean the following:

Sequence 111. You are here to create magic for others! Seek your magic within – you have all the tools you need to make things happen; your thoughts manifest reality. Step into your role as a spiritual teacher and enhance the faith of others. Demonstrate what is possible when you use your own inherent gifts.

Sequence 222. You have the ability to magnify the energy of others! You create a sacred and Divine balance between Masculine and Feminine forces. Seek balance in duality and find healing in union with "the other". You are beloved – your other is always there, in spirit or human form. Seek what is missing from your life, for it is also seeking you.

Sequence 333. You are capable of overcoming any obstacle in your path. When you doubt yourself, remember all the tiny miracles you have manifested over time. See the world through the lens of a carefree child. Cultivate a sense of wonder and let it carry you through periods of struggle and hardship. Life always wins. Love always wins.

Sequence 444. You are creating a foundation for your dreams. Surrender your fears and trust that the universe is supporting you, encouraging you, and providing the structure you need to create what you desire. Give thanks and leave room for the universe to work its magic on your behalf.

Sequence 555. You are attracting prosperity and wealth; keep your arms outstretched to continue receiving and integrating. At times you will be called to sacrifice in service of the greater good. Remember to trust that your angels are always giving you extra support.

Sequence 666. You are a peace-bearer on a quest for truth and deep connection. Your empathic ability to heal others also helps you understand your own trauma and grief. Choose to provide care and kindness over service and sacrifice.

Sequence 777. You have come full circle on your sacred soul path toward wisdom and truth. You have the ability to understand and work in rhythm with the natural cycles of life and death in order to find peace. Keep going! Your relationship with Source is stronger and more meaningful now.

Sequence 888. Abundance is your birthright! You naturally attract prosperity and find it easy to magnetize money and opportunity to increase your wealth. Expand what you possess and accumulate resources in service of the highest good. Connect with others with similar interests and find ways to selflessly share the riches you enjoy today.

Sequence 999. A cycle is ending and subsequently, a new cycle is beginning. You are here to help others ascend to higher levels of spiritual awareness. Consider the role that endings play in your life and how you can honor them in a powerful and intentional way. The completion of your sacred journey has opened the way for the work of your soul to unfold.

There are also different meanings for other signs...

Feathers- They are in our path at just the right moment to offer love, validation, and comfort.

Clouds- They say I'm right here and I love you.

Red Cardinals- While I didn't see a red cardinal, my snow globe with red cardinals turned itself on during one of the hardest days of grieving. Thanksgiving is my favorite holiday thus, a very hard one to be without Cody. I made it through the second Thanksgiving without him only because I was so busy. With everyone gone, Thanksgiving put away and Christmas put up, I was not in the mood to turn on the beautiful snow globe that I had just bought for Cody really, it is a red lantern with a log cabin, Aspen trees with two red cardinals in the trees. It lights up and silver glitter circles around. My dad and I turned it on Thanksgiving Day and sat staring at it. However, on Friday, when my grief and deep sorrow hit me as I was really missing Cody, I didn't even feel like turning it on. So, off it stayed. Then Saturday morning as I came out into the family room, there it was turned on. The only light in the room. Beautiful! It took my breath away. I asked Duane and Kaylee both if they had turned it on. No. I even begged them to just tell me the truth as they like to play tricks on me. They swore it was not them. Then it hit me as I looked up the meaning of a red cardinal as a sign…it symbolizes the importance of faith. The loved one is letting us know that the spirit is with us to remind us that passion, warmth, and strength are available to us especially when we are in a time of dark grief. WOW!

Hawks, Crows, and other birds- They help us see the big picture, bring luck and joy.

Music- It's like receiving a kiss or an "I love you" from the other side.

Electrical Phenomena- Just trying to say, "I'm here."

One sign that I have never had from Cody is having him appear in a dream (probably because for almost two years I didn't sleep). However, Duane, Kaylee, and some of Cody's friends have experienced having him appear to them in a dream. Kaylee had a very vivid dream she shared with me…

She said it was the weekend of May 26, 2018, when we were in Flaming Gorge, Utah. We planned the trip to celebrate Cody. Kaylee met us later that day with some of her friends on their way back from Colorado. Here is what she told me…

It was just like any other night I have had over the last 2 months,

every night just before bed I would replay the worst day of my life in my

head. It was extremely hard for me to black out the vivid flashbacks

from the night my brother died. This particular night I was the last one

to bed as I crawled in the bunkbeds at the back of the trailer that Cody

and I would sleep in when we went camping. It was like I was 13 again

and life was still happy. This night I remember waking up with a warm,

intense sensation. It was around 1:00 AM, about the same time we lost

Cody. It was the most vivid dream I have ever had in my life. In the

dream, I was walking into the Lucerne Valley Marina and I see this tall

skinny guy standing there with his hat backwards and I say to myself

that sure looks a lot like my brother. A few seconds later the man turns

around and I remember my eyes getting big once I realized who it was. It

was actually Cody! I could not believe it. He starts running at me, hugs

me so tight, then picked me up, and spun me around. I was so happy to

see my brother again and he looked so happy like the weight of the

world was lifted off his shoulders. He said to me, "I love you Kaylee, you

have to know I didn't do this on purpose, it was an accident please

forgive me." As I looked him in the eyes I could tell he meant what he

said. I hugged him again and said I loved him and that he looked happy, to which he said he felt comfort again. I wanted that moment to last

forever just so I could have my happy loving brother back just a little

longer, but he said he had to go. I watched him walk out the door. I ran

to follow him, but as soon as I opened the door he was gone and that is

when I woke up. I shot straight out of my bed and looked around

because I swear it felt real like Cody was actually there. I blinked a

couple more times realizing it was a dream and laid back down trying to

fall back asleep again in hopes he would come back. This was the most

real- life feeling dream I have ever had and Cody gave that to me. I

suddenly felt closure. I knew that he was okay, he loved me, and I will

never forget the warm feeling I got when I woke up. I love Cody for

giving me this memory.

A short time after that Duane told me about a similar dream

that he had about Cody. It was also at Flaming Gorge at the Lucerne

Valley Marina, he had walked into the little store and looked up over

toward the fishing lures and saw Cody. Cody was wearing one of his hats

and a hoodie and he gave him a peace sign and a smile then he was

gone.

I have celebrated every sign that Cody has given me and I

always say, "Thank you, son,"

because he has truly helped me to carry on without him. Honestly, there have been many times where I have not wanted to, but I guess he is helping to guide me through this life on earth and carry out God's plan for me whatever that is.

The only reason messages are missed is doubt. Our loved ones want to stay connected to us. Therefore, I challenge you to open your heart and mind then trust. Believe in the afterlife connections.

It has helped me through the grief process and brought me tears of joy. The messages and signs from my son are a blessing and part of our unbreakable bond.

Chapter 13

See You Again

"Be the things you love most about the people who are gone."

~Unknown

The things I love most about Cody are his smile, laugh, fun-

loving spirit, love of adventure, love of children, caring heart for others,

love of fashion, love for cooking, love for family and friends, and love for

entertainment. So, just as the quote says, I am going to spend my life

being and doing the things that I love most about my son, who is gone. I am going to live life for him and do the things that I know he would have wanted to do, but didn't get a chance to do. So far, I think that we are doing a pretty good job at this. Two birthdays have passed since Cody's death and on the first one, we went to dinner at Red Lobster where he always liked to go and ordered what he would have ordered. On the second one, which would have been his 28th birthday, we went snowmobiling and stayed in a cabin. He would have loved it. As a family, we will continue to celebrate Cody and think about what he would have wanted to do.

Duane now has a new duck hunting partner, Kaylee, I know that Cody is smiling down on them every time that they go duck hunting. I know that he is glad that Duane didn't give up hunting and that Kaylee is going with him. She got new waders and a shotgun. I'm sure Cody is so proud. I can hear him saying, "Way to go, sissy." Another sign of what is meant to be, Duane and Cody had always talked about buying a new duck boat well, Duane just did from a man named Cody and as he drove away with the boat, you can guess which song started to play on the radio, I kid you not. Duane believes in signs now, too.

See You Again

It's been a long day without you, my friend
And I'll tell you all about it when I see you again
We've come a long way from where we began
Oh I'll tell you all about it when I see you again
When I see you again

Damn, who knew all the planes we flew
Good things we've been through
That I'll be standing right here
Talking to you about another path I
Know we loved to hit the road and laugh
But something told me that it wouldn't last
Had to switch up look at things different see the bigger picture
Those were the days hard work forever pays now I see you in a
better place

How could we not talk about family when family's all that we got?
Everything I went through you were standing there by my side
And now you gonna be with me for the last ride

It's been a long day without you, my friend
And I'll tell you all about it when I see you again
We've come a long way from where we began
Oh I'll tell you all about it when I see you again
When I see you again

First you both go out your way
And the vibe is feeling strong and what's
Small turn to a friendship, a friendship
Turn into a bond and that bond will never
Be broken and the love will never get lost
And when brotherhood come first then the line
Will never be crossed established it on our own
When that line had to be drawn and that line is what
We reach so remember me when I'm gone

How could we not talk about family when family's all that we got?

Everything I went through you were standing there by my side
And now you gonna be with me for the last ride

So let the light guide your way hold every memory
As you go and every road you take will always lead you home

It's been a long day without you, my friend
And I'll tell you all about it when I see you again
We've come a long way from where we began
Oh I'll tell you all about it when I see you again
When I see you again

We will see our dear son again. I cannot wait. I can picture that

day in my mind clearly. I often listen to the song, " I Can Only Imagine,"

and I picture Cody standing right next to Jesus and I will go running into

their arms. He will have a giant smile on his face (this is how I always see

him now) and my heart will be filled with overwhelming joy!

We will have so much to catch up on, but he already knows

what has gone on with us, it will be what he has to show me in Heaven.

That is a time that I truly look forward to! Until I see you again my dear,

sweet son I will live my life to the fullest the best that I can and with

your help I will do my best to honor all of the things that I love the most

about you.

Chapter 14

Life Rolls On

"Forever in our hearts"

~Unknown

Some of you may be asking "Why"? Why would she write this book about her son and put herself out there like that? Well, I will tell you why... my son's story needs to be told. If by telling his story, I can help even one person, then my "why" has been a success! I need to tell his story not only to help others, but to celebrate the amazing person that he was when his addiction was not ruling his life.

I feel that it is my duty and new mission in life to help people understand the disease of addiction and erase the stigma. We need to look at others differently, perhaps with a lens of understanding rather than one of judgement. This disease is killing too many people and the reach of it is affecting far too many families. Every human life is of value and important.

It is devastating to lose a family member under any circumstance and I am certainly not here to tell you that any one death is harder to grieve than another however, I do know that the loss of a child is absolutely heartbreaking and is a pain that is so horrendous, you never truly recover.

I am not the same person and I never will be. I have a totally different outlook on life. Life is short. I need to live it. I know that I will always have pain. I have it daily. However, I choose happy because that is what Cody would have wanted me to do. I am living for him. I need to live for my husband, my daughter, my parents, and my siblings. I need to live for myself.

Yes, I have needed time to heal, try to erase the guilt, and grieve, but I have come to learn this… I may never know some of the answers and that is something that I am just going to have to accept. It was God's plan. I did my best. It may not have been good enough, but I can't change it. What I can do is celebrate Cody's life and keep his memory alive. Instead of asking the wrong questions about what I could have done differently, I can ask the right questions like, " Now, what am I going to do about it?" I can spend more time with family and friends. I can do the best at my job. I can check things of my bucket list. I can be the best version of myself. Most importantly, I can spread the word about addiction and be an advocate for the disease. With that being said, I'd like to share some thoughts on the opioid crisis.

Facts, Fury, and Forgiveness

Facts

All through Cody's struggle with addiction we all found that we needed to educate ourselves on many things…signs of drug use, what different drugs and paraphernalia looked like, symptoms, effects, and

213

side effects of drugs, addiction and withdrawal, and who/where to get help from. Since my son's death, I think it's important to start with some facts and statistics about opioids and the crisis in our country. This has become known as the worst crisis in American history. The CDC estimates the current total economic burden at $78.5 billion due to the costs of health care, lost worker productivity, addiction treatment, crime, and the justice system.

Some of these facts you may already know some you may not and sadly they are changing for the worse every year. In the 1990s pharmaceutical companies reassured the medical communities that patients wouldn't become addicted to the medications classified as opioids class so, they were prescribed at higher rates. Now, it is known that some people can become addicted to opioids in 5-7 days. In the United States, every 11-12 minutes someone dies of an opioid overdose. That's 130 people per day. The number of women using opioids during pregnancy has risen 70% between 2015 -2017 and in 2012 there was a baby born every 25 minutes addicted to opioids.

Here are some statistics according to the Kaiser Family Foundation, in 2017, there were 70,237 deaths in the United States due to drug overdoses. Of those deaths, 68% of them were opioid overdoses for a total of 47,600. The majority of opioid users are men. Among the opioid overdoses in 2017; 37,113 of them were white, 5,513 were black, and 3,932 were Hispanic.

This crisis is everywhere, in every state, in the big cities, and in the small towns. It knows no social class as it affects both rich and poor. From the homeless to the multi-homeowners and the corporate executives to the unemployed. It has no boundaries. People considered to have high religious morals and people with no religious beliefs are affected just the same. Your neighbors, coworkers, friends, distant family members, , close family members, and even your precious child. The ranking of states is always changing I'm sure, but according to the CDC in 2015 the top ten states for drug overdose deaths were in order starting with number one: West Virginia, New Hampshire, Kentucky, Ohio, Rhode Island, Pennsylvania, New Mexico, **Utah**, and Tennessee. Utah, we are at number nine (I have seen other articles where Utah has been number seven) and in our state, Tooele, where we live is number one, according to an article in The Salt Lake Tribune, by Kelly Gifford on May 31, 2017.

If you've made it through this far reading all of this information, I hope that these facts are disturbing to you and that you realize what a crisis this is. Some of you may have already known this and feel like I do...the need to speak up and make people aware. Some may feel even more passionate like I do and want to do whatever we can to help and find solutions to this crisis. I also hope that you are feeling some empathy for the individuals struggling with this disease and their families, who have been impacted. I know, however, some of you may be angry and feeling like it was their choice and they brought it upon themselves so, why is it your problem? I understand that you may feel that way, but I want to share something my daughter saw...it may or may not help you understand/change your opinion.

Drug Use: *Choice*

Addiction: *Disease*

Unprotected Sex: Choice

STD: *Disease*

Use of Tobacco :   *Choice*

Cancer: *Disease*

Use of Alcohol: *Choice*

Alcoholism: *Disease*

Lack of Exercise/Unhealthy Diet: Choice

Obesity: Leads to many diseases and disorders

If you are overweight; use tobacco or alcohol products; have unprotected sex...

You can stop shaming recovering addicts. Your poor decisions haven't resulted in consequences......YET.

Yes, addiction is a disease. Let me tell you some things about heroin that doctors and scientists have found as they have studied it effects on the brain. First of all, a few quick statistics about heroin, 80% of heroin users first misused prescription opioids. Heroin overdoses in the United States have increased 5 times the number from 2010 to 2017.

Heroin is a very dangerous drug. Heroin is in the opioid class of drugs with the main active ingredient in it being morphine. It comes in many shapes and sizes. There are many types found in the United States including white, brown, and black tar heroin. You can smoke, swallow, snort, and shoot it, which is the most dangerous. It is known to be highly addictive even after one use. Long term use can cause the brain to stop making its own endorphins, which results in the in the addict's body becoming barely capable of managing small amounts of pain or discomfort. Heroin changes how the brain functions, which alters a person's mood, perception, and consciousness. It has been associated with deteriorations of white matter in the brain causing the addict to have poor decision making, self-regulation, and responding to stress abilities.

When someone uses heroin, they have a quick feeling of euphoria, pleasure and relief from psychological and physical pain sensations. This first hit and the sense of euphoria only lasts a few minutes, but then the person begins to feel drowsy and appears to nod off. They are sluggish, have slurred speech, and appear confused. They often describe this stage of the high as a warm, cozy and relaxed feeling. Breathing and heart rate both slow down. This can last for a few hours. The brain is altered and withdrawal symptoms occur within a few hours to ten hours after use. These symptoms may include: a strong craving for more, muscle and bone pain, chills, vomiting, trouble sleeping, restlessness, heart and lung problems, diarrhea, moodiness, stomach cramps, sweating, runny nose, fever, sweating, muscle spasms, nausea, increased heart rate and blood pressure.

.

I will end there with the drug facts and statistics. I know more that I want to about the subject. However, I am a person that believes that education is the key to understanding each other and to solving problems. Knowledge is power. Sometimes it may be hard to face the fact and there may be some things that we do not necessarily want to know about, but we cannot always turn a blind eye and ignore things that affect a whole society.

I have recently been listening to the Project Recovery podcasts by Casey Scott. They are very powerful and enlightening. In one of the episodes, as I listened to Welterweight MMA fighter, Court Magee, I appreciated his honesty and his mission to spread awareness about addiction. That is what I now believe that I need to do. He talked about the Devil's Cocktail, which is a combination of alcohol, pills, weed, Xanax, and cocaine. Wow. It took me back to when I read my son's coroner's report. I was in shock. It's so hard to believe and sad that a person feels that they need to have a mixture of those things to make them feel better or I guess not feel anything. It's heart breaking that people, including my own son are that sad and in that much pain. As I said before, I am not embarrassed of my son, I loved him and I still love him with my whole heart, but for whatever reason, I feel it is now my duty to share his story - our story, both the good and the bad so, that hopefully other families do not have to go through what we have been through. I do not care if I am looked at differently or judged for it because it is what it is and it happened for a reason. I will spread awareness and kindness from now on to help all of the people that I can.

Fury

I'll admit that at first Duane and Kaylee were very, very angry. Kaylee new the passwords to all of Cody's social media accounts so, she was able to see all of his calls, read all of his texts, Facebook messenger messages, other social media posts, locations he had been and any other history in his phone. We have a home security system with outside cameras so, even though we had turned his phone over to the police and they were investigating. We did our own digging and we had it figured out who, when, where, and a general timeline of when he purchased the drugs. I read everything as well because of course, I wanted the facts and I just wanted to know. I had to piece it all together. I'm not going to get into any further details on this.

I know that they will always be angry and rightfully so. Everyone has a right to their feelings. I know that as the weeks went on and we didn't hear anything about the case they continued to be angry.

I think it is natural to feel angry with yourself and that is a part of the healing process, if you can ever totally heal from this, which I'm 100% certain that you cannot. I've already shared the feelings of guilt with you which go along with being angry at yourself or at each other as parents for not doing more. I've found however, that none of that does anyone any good.

Sometimes, I'll admit I find myself angry at God. Right after Cody's death, I turned to my Pastor and he was amazing. He met me at Starbucks and we talked for over an hour. He made me feel a lot better and he suggested some books to read. One book that I read was, The Shack, I really liked that book. It gave me some comfort, hope, and peace. I was questioning Cody's faith and my own faith, but after reading that book, I felt well again and a new confidence that my son was in Heaven waiting for me.

Forgiveness

Forgiveness is the intentional and voluntary process of letting go of negative emotions regarding an offense. It's not seeking revenge. It's not wasting your time and energy dwelling on something that has already happened and cannot be change. Let it go.

I think that I had an easier time with not being furious at the people that we know played a role in Cody's death. I do understand that he is the one that used the drugs that night. He made that choice. I understand addiction and I understood him. I don't like it, and I don't fully understand God's plan, but I know that being angry won't help anything.

I learned the power of forgiveness a few years ago. Since then, I can honestly say that I harbor no feelings of hatred toward anyone. I used to have one or two people that I was always obsessing about because they had hurt me in some way, or now that I think about it, I was probably jealous of them. When I think of all of the time and effort wasted on those thoughts and feelings now, it's just plain silly to me.

Cody and I talked about this a lot. He wasn't quite to the point that I was in forgiveness, but he was 26. We had this in common however, we both had a good friend that we had for years that we did everything with, who pretty much dumped us. We both had introduced our friend to another friend and they became friends with each other and started to just leave us out and not invite us. So, Cody and I knew how each other felt. I got over it though, I came to a point where I looked around and saw what was most important to me, my family. I decided that I didn't need a friend like that and even though I had always been that person, who wouldn't dare eat lunch at a restraunt alone, it was okay. I started to go shopping alone and do things on my own or with Cody and Kaylee. It was great. I let it go. I can honestly say that I truly wish everyone I meet the very best and I choose to not be angry at anyone. If someone does something to me, I try to understand the "why" and look at all perspectives and I'm honest about my feelings. I do not judge others and I try to look at everyone's perspective on things. Of course, I don't always agree, but that's okay. I even forgive the people that sold or gave my son the drugs that caused his overdose. I won't forget it, but I'm not going to waste my time and energy full of fury. I choose to forgive.

Here is the important thing about forgiveness, we need to forgive ourselves when we know that at the time, we tried our best. We need to forgive the addict and their choice. We need to forgive others including those that gave them the drug and move on because we cannot change it. In a book I recently read, *The Happiness Advantage*, by Shawn Achor, this called "Falling Up." We can survive trauma and choose to take a path that helps us move forward.

Afterword

Hopes and Dreams

Psalm 71:14 But I will hope continually and will praise you yet more and more

"A dream doesn't become reality through magic; it takes sweat, determination and hard work." ~Collin Powell

It is my hope that Cody has forgiven himself. I know that he may not have remembered every action and every word that was said, but I know the guilt and pain that he felt when he would relapse, or when something would happen. I forgive him and I hope that he is at peace with himself now, knowing that we all know that everyone did their best, not perfect and not without mistakes, but their best at the moment.

I came across a letter that I want to include. It is very powerful.

Cody and I would read it together several times. Unfortunately, there is

a lot of truth in it. He had multiple copies of this letter. He would get

one after every rehab, every time he went to counseling, I know that he

didn't just nonchalantly cast it to the side because we talked about it.

One time he taped it to the mirror on his dresser. Sadly, the letter came

true and he lost the battle, but not without a fight. He did fight and I am

proud of him for that.

LETTER FROM YOUR ADDICTION

Dear Friend:

I've come to visit one again. I love to see you suffer mentally, physically, spiritually and socially. I want to have you restless so, you can never relax. I want you jumpy, nervous and anxious. I want to make you agitated and irritable so everything and everybody makes you uncomfortable. I want you to be depressed and confused so, that you can't think clearly or positively. I want to make you hate everything and everybody, especially yourself. I want you to feel guilty and remorseful for the things you have done in the past that you'll never be able to let go. I want to make you angry and hateful toward the world for the way it is and the way you are. I want you to feel sorry for yourself and blame everything, but your addiction for the way things are. I want you to be deceitful and untrustworthy, and to manipulate and con as many people as possible. I want to make you fearful and paranoid for no reason at all and I want you to wake up during all hours of the night screaming for me. You know you can't sleep without me; I'm even in your dreams.

I want to be the first thing you wake up to every morning and the last thing you touch before you black out. I would rather kill you, but I'll be happy enough if I can put you back in the hospital, another institution, or jail. But you know that I'll still waiting for you when you come out. I love to watch you slowly going insane. I love to see all the physical damage that I'm causing you. I can't help but sneer and chuckle when you shiver and shake, when you freeze and sweat at the same time, when you wake up with your blankets soaking wet.

It's amazing how much destruction I can do to your internal organs while at the same time work on your brain, destroying it bit by bit. I deeply appreciate how much you sacrifice for me. The countless good jobs you have sacrificed for me. All the fine friends that you deeply cared for - you gave them up for me. And what's more, for the ones you turned against yourself because of your inexcusable actions - I am more grateful.

And especially your loved ones, your family, and the most important people in the world to you. You even threw them away for me. I cannot express in words the gratitude I have for the loyalty you have for me. You sacrificed all these beautiful things in your life just to devote yourself completely to me, but do not despair my friend, for on me you can always depend. For after you have lost all these things, you can still depend on me to take even more. You can depend on me to keep you in living hell, to keep your mind, body and soul. FOR I WILL NOT BE SATISFIED UNTIL YOU ARE DEAD MY FRIEND.

Faithfully Yours,

Your addiction and drug of choice

(Author Unknown)

Kaylee asked me to take her picture because she was going to put it on a blog. We both follow different sites about addiction. I'm really proud of her for the way she has carried herself and tried to chase her hopes and dreams while at the same time accepting the loss of her brother. She sent me a text asking if she could post and share the following... Of course, I said yes! Neither of us are embarrassed about Cody, rather, we would like to share our story to help others. Every time Kaylee reads something about an overdose, she will comment back to me about how similar the stories are. The personalities of the loved one that was lost, the circumstances that the families went through, and the facts about addiction. One thing that we both agree on passionately is that there is still a stigma and it's time for it to be done.

I'm not sure why, or if the day will ever come when the stigma of drug addiction and overdose is more understood. I hope that I live to see that day. I remember when we didn't talk about someone dying by suicide or even dare to talk about mental illness in one's family. Now, with suicide being a leading cause of death and mental illness at the forefront of concern in our society, they are discussed more and even becoming somewhat accepted. However, drugs are still a no, no that are not talked about. It's interesting when something is posted on

Facebook about it, people very rarely give it a like, share, or even read it. It is becoming one of the most common killers, which affects many families, but we are still living in the "no, not in my family" mentality with a stigma attached. Many people believe drug addiction as a choice that "they" can and should just stop.

Here is Kaylee's beautifully written post. We appreciate the heart felt comments she received and our love goes out to all of those affected by this crisis.

August 31st International Overdose Awareness day.

A day I never believed I would "celebrate" but a day that should be recognized. I've now been a part of this day for 2 years. I have struggled in many different ways with acknowledging addiction as a disease. I will admit I never saw it like that until I watched it consume my brother. I watched him change into a completely different person. Never did I ever think anything would ever happen to him I thought that he was always going to be there. Until everything was ripped away faster than you could blink. Everything came crashing down like an avalanche. My past, future and present are now gone. The person I knew that was supposed to be in my life until we were both gray and old is gone forever. You hear all of these people call addicts "druggies" "junkies" "worthless" did any of you actually think they wanted to live their lives like this. The answer is simple NO! You won't know how hard the daily struggle is until you see it or witness it firsthand.

There are 192 deaths a day from drug overdoses. In one year, there are 72,000 deaths from an overdose. These numbers surpass car accidents and gun violence things that everyone is aware of. But people put shame and a stigma on drug overdose when there shouldn't be. We should become more aware this stopping the epidemic.

August 31st
On this day we wear purple to remember those we have lost to this epidemic.

I wear purple for my brother, Cody Gillette

Cody Gillette was born December 6th, 1991 as soon as he graced this world, he would always have an amazing strong driven passion for anything and everything he loved.

I just wanted to say a couple things about my brother. In my own opinion I would say that God's greatest gift is his having a brother. Cody was always by my side since before I was born. He helped me in so many ways. When I was little, I barely said three words. Cody helped me come out of my shell. Cody and I are 18 months apart in age. When we went to preschool I wouldn't go to school unless Cody was there with me so he ended up staying with me another year. I wish my mom would have let him stay another year cause then when my grandma forgot me, I wouldn't have been so terrified I would've had my big bro by my side.

My dad's love of the outdoors passed on to Cody and they both tried to pass it on to me it worked for a couple of years but then I decided to be more of a girl. I remember the first time they took me rabbit hunting and I "shot" my first rabbit but I can guarantee it was really Cody because he was more excited than I was he was screaming and yelling jumping on me. But I think it was really Cody who shot it unless my rapid-fire style paid off.

From sitting in a backyard duck blind and yelling "Take em!", To me and my best friend London on all fours pretending to be deer and Cody shooting us with a fake bow and arrow. To peeing in my waders and my love of animals hunting was just too much for me!

Growing up in the horseshoe we had the best times playing backyard baseball and kick the can with all the neighbors. Being added to the work force before I even knew what that meant. He would send London and I up to the golf course with some golf balls and told us to sell as many as we could and that he would be right back leaving us with the hard work while he went home to eat a pizza with mom.

One thing about myself is that I think I am pretty good at keeping secrets but Cody never kept secrets from me. I wish I would have told on him that night I saw him doing something he shouldn't be or all those times I covered for him when he never made it home. I question myself everyday did I do the right thing, or should I have told on him maybe it would have stopped his addiction before it got bad. Honestly, I just wanted to be that sister who didn't tattle tale on their brother I wanted him to think I was cool. Which it might have cost me my brother? During the dark times of his addiction I could barely recognize this person he had become. I knew the man staring at me was not my brother. I knew my brother wouldn't steal or hurt me like this man has done. I screamed so many times to myself please just stop Cody please I just want my brother back! It took me a long time to understand addiction it really made me mad the things he would do and I never understood why. Why he just wouldn't quit be done with this black hole that was destroying his life. I had to step back it was painful losing pieces of your brother of your best friend the person you looked up to growing up. I saw what it was doing to my parents and I didn't know how to stop it. I kept thinking once he hits is rock bottom, he'll turn it around I know it. We just had to figure out what that rock bottom was... March 1st the horrible thing we all knew could happened but didn't want to ever believe it could happen to us actually happened. I wish I could forget everything from that day from that minute and just rewind 10 years and tell my brother to just stop don't take that turn around go home do anything but that Cody please.

I lost a big piece of myself that day a piece I'll never get back. A brother that I'll never get to share my life with. An Uncle that will never see his nieces/nephews. A future I don't know how I will go on without but I know I have to for him. Drug overdose is not something to judge someone on or throw shame. Everyone is still a human no matter their choices no one is worthless.

This is why I wear purple to remember the amazing person my brother was. To remember we are not alone. To remember the other who have lost their lives. To remember the people struggling to cope with that lost.

Cody,

Thank you for being you thank you for making my laugh thank you for protecting me thank you for being my brother. I love you.

#iwearpurple #overdoseawareness2019 #mybrotherskeeper#siblingsl eftbehind #whatsleftbehind

Last year, the first year after Cody had passed, I had company that I hadn't seen in many years staying with me to visit my dad, whose dementia had worsened. This year, I am recovering from knee surgery, but our hope is that next year, Kaylee and I will run in the 3K and join in the activities at the Utah State Capitol on August 31st. We will make sure to submit a picture of Cody for the Utah "Remembrance Video," for International Overdose Day, and my dream is that this book will be published and helping others find some comfort or inspiration to share their stories. Thank you. Bless you.

I want to list a few final thoughts, tips, and possible suggestions that I have for those of you who have experienced the trauma of addiction in anyway. Some of these have helped me to have the

courage and hope to carry on. They have been a way of healing for me.

My way of healing has been to...

- o Read many books
- o I still talk to Cody
- o I talk about Cody
- o I wrote this book
- o I write in a journal
- o My job being around kids is a happy place
- o I went skydiving
- o I went mountain climbing
- o I rode the damn bull
- o I am checking things off my bucket list
- o I started the HOPE support group
- o I am going to set up a foundation
- o I am going to organize a community awareness and charity event
- o I am planning on setting up a scholarship in Cody's name
- o I stay as positive as I can every day

I am not an expert on grief by any means, I do not have a psychology degree, nor do I pretend to have all of the answers on how others feel or react to situations. I am speaking from my own experience to hopefully, shed some light on what may be "normal" if there is such a thing in the grief process. Maybe you will read this and make a connection.

Through the first year of our tragedy of losing our son there were many questions like:

- How do we even move forward? How will we even survive without him? Do we even want to?

- Who is to blame?

- My whole life revolved around my son. So, now what do I do? Who am I now?

- Did he suffer as he was dying?

- Is Cody in Heaven?

- Am I okay? Is what I'm doing- the way I'm acting and feeling normal?

- Will our marriage survive this?

- Am I giving enough attention to Kaylee and Duane?

- How do I help others?

Here are some of the answers that I found through reading many books, talking with others that had gone through the loss of a child, seeking spiritual advice, looking inside myself, and doing research:

- Grief takes time-you need to try to move beyond it-people go through the stages at different times and in different ways

- Learn the stages of grief-list them and get an explanation

- You need to move beyond the guilt and put the regrets, what ifs and if onlys behind you

- After the sheer devastation and shock, I'll admit that I felt a small wave of relief that the battle was over and my son was no longer in pain and could be in peace

- Yes, he is in Heaven

- My whole life revolved around him by worrying and lying awake at night wondering if he was safe, waiting for a text to know that he was alive and well, constantly checking on him, his constant needing of me, but now I will live for me and for him I will do the things that I know he would want me to do and that he would have wanted to do!

- The need to know all of what happened-As far as I can tell Cody's death was like going to sleep
- I have found common grief partners not just in my family, but in other mother's in my HOPE support group. We can meet, talk, and understand each other totally.
- Our marriage is having its ups and downs. I won't lie it's rough. I know we can make it through.
- I continue to focus on the good memories like Cody's smile, laugh, the sound of the ice maker when he would get up at night
- We are making new memories that Cody would have liked
- I try to help others

- I keep his memory alive - his room is still intact and more of a "shrine" or a sanctuary for us to go and reflect

My wish for you is that no matter where you are at in your life right now, that you move forward with the courage and determination to follow your hopes and dreams. It's not too late. I am a firm believer that anything is possible. I wish you the very best. As life rolls on please remember to be kind to others, we don't know everyone's story. Thank you for reading mine.

Acknowledgements

Thank you first and foremost to my husband and daughter, who are amazing. I love you very much. Thank you to my parents, my two brothers, and all of our family members. You are all very special to me. I cherish all of your love and support. To all of my friends and co-workers, you have been my saving grace through all of this. Thank you to my whole community for your continued support.

Special thanks to Jordan, Kanyon, Kevin, and Scott for their very special stories told of Cody and used in the book with their permission.

Thank you to all of Cody's friends. He loved you all very much.

Thank you to Cody's coaches Steve Branch and Eddie Clements for their positive influence in Cody's life.

Thank you to Cole Houghton, Tate Mortuary, Mike and Cindy Hollar, everyone that helped with Cody's funeral preparations along with support before and after the funeral.

Thanks to all of the parents who share their children with me every day by sending them to school each allowing me to be an influence in their lives and giving me a reason to smile.

Thank you to all of the parents I know who have also lost a child and have shared their stories and grief with me. I understand the best that I can and I love you. Thank you to the parents I do not know who have lost a child, but have written a book, wrote a song, or spoke about you loss in some way. I cannot tell you how grateful I am to you for helping me grieve.

Finally, thank you to all of you that continued to encourage me to write this book, helped me in the editing and publishing process. Most of all thank you to all of you that have chosen to read it.

References and Resources

Resources

I encourage anyone that is struggling with addiction to contact their local mental health departments for advice. You can also do a Google search for free rehab centers. The search will most likely pop up with several choices that may or may not direct you to free resources, but most of them will have a number that you can call to speak with someone for immediate help.

You can always go to your local hospital to detox and receive help. Please rely on family and friends. There are also the groups like Alcoholics Anonymous and Narcotics Anonymous that are free.

References

Kalifa, Wiz. Puth, Charlie. perf. *See You Again.* Song. 2015

McGraw, Tim. perf. *Live Like You Are Dying.* Song. 2004

Gillette, Cody. Gillette, Kaylee. Gillette, Duane. www.facebook.com @Utah Wildboys

Utah Wildboys Foundation

Ragan, Lyn. (2014). *Signs From the Afterlife.* Atlanta, GA

Achor, Shawn. (2010). *The Happiness Advantage.* Currency Books, New York

Wachs, Stephanie Wittels. (2018). *Everything is Horrible and Wonderful.* Sourcebooks: Naperville, Illinois

CDC-Centers for Disease Control and Prevention- https://www.cdc.gov

www.kff.org -Kaiser Family Foundation nonprofit website provides health information

National Institute on Drug Abuse-https://www.drugabuse.gov

www.opioidsthetruth.com

Podcast- Project Recovery- Scott, Casey. (2019). *Project Recovery*. KSL Podcasts: Salt Lake City, UT

Angel numbers-www.sagegoddess.com

ABOUT THE AUTHOR

Angie Gillette was born in South Dakota and now resides in Stansbury Park, Utah with her husband Duane, daughter Kaylee, and two grand dogs Avery and Gracie. Angie loves people and especially children, besides being the mother of her own two children, she has influenced the lives of thousands of others. Since the age of five, all she ever wanted to be was a teacher. This is her 29th year in education. She has been an elementary teacher, an elementary principal, and a secondary assistant principal.

Angie loves fashion especially shoes. Her hobbies include shopping, reading, and traveling. The thing to Angie is spending time with her family. She loves adventure, trying new things, and being around people.

Angie's story is one of honesty and strength. Her book is a tribute to her late son, Cody Gillette, who lost his battle with addiction at the age of 26. She wants to share her story to honor him and to help others understand the battle of addiction. Also, to let other parents and families know that they are not alone in this epidemic and that life can roll on, it may not be easy, but with kindness, understanding instead of judgment, and empathy toward others we can all learn to appreciate each other.

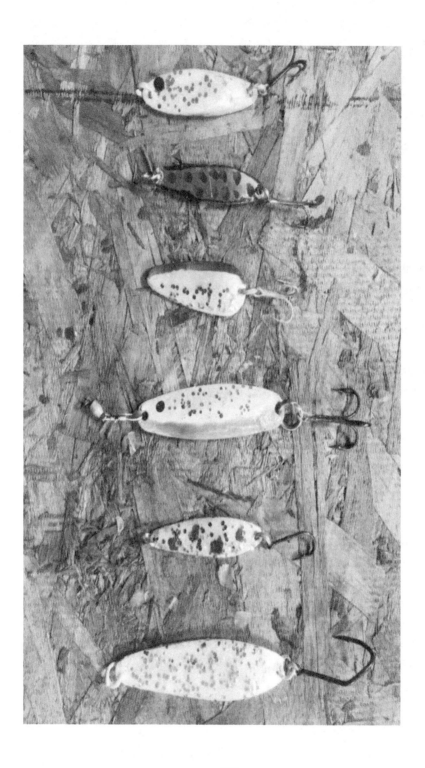

Made in the USA
Middletown, DE
11 January 2024

47604081R00149